Zombies, Consumption, and Satire in Capcom's Dead Rising

This book explores the relationship between video games and satire through an in-depth examination of Capcom's *Dead Rising* series, which alludes to, recontextualises, and builds upon George A. Romero's filmic satire on American consumer culture, *Dawn of the Dead.*

Proposing a taxonomy of videoludic satire, this book details how video games can communicate satire through their virtual environments, their characters, their audio, the way they frame the passage of time, and the outcomes of in-game choices that their players can make. By applying this taxonomy to the *Dead Rising* series, this book presents a compelling case for how video games can function as instruments for social commentary and indicators of ideological tensions.

This unique and insightful study will interest students and scholars of media studies, video game studies, satire, visual culture, and zombie studies.

Connor Jackson (PhD, Edge Hill University) is a Student Learning Administrator at Liverpool Hope University, UK. His research focuses on how video games reinforce and challenge ideas about the world and human behaviour. He is also interested in horror in relation to and beyond video games.

Routledge Advances in Game Studies

Videogames and Agency
Bettina Bódi

Posthuman Gaming
Avatars, Gamers, and Entangled Subjectivities
Poppy Wilde

Traveling through Video Games
Tom van Nuenen

Metagames: Games about Games
Agata Waszkiewicz

On Soulsring Worlds
Narrative Complexity, Digital Communities,
and Interpretation in *Dark Souls* and *Elden Ring*
Marco Caracciolo

Asian Histories and Heritages in Video Games
Edited by Yowei Kang, Kenneth C.C. Yang, Michał Mochocki, Jakub Majewski & Paweł Schreiber

Central and Eastern European Histories and Heritages in Video Games
Edited by Michał Mochocki, Paweł Schreiber, Jakub Majewski, and Yaraslau I. Kot

Zombies, Consumption, and Satire in Capcom's Dead Rising
Connor Jackson

For more information about this series, please visit: https://www.routledge.com/Routledge-Advances-in-Game-Studies/book-series/RAIGS

Zombies, Consumption, and Satire in Capcom's Dead Rising

Connor Jackson

Routledge
Taylor & Francis Group
LONDON AND NEW YORK

First published 2025
by Routledge
4 Park Square, Milton Park, Abingdon, Oxon OX14 4RN

and by Routledge
605 Third Avenue, New York, NY 10158

Routledge is an imprint of the Taylor & Francis Group, an informa business

British Library Cataloguing-in-Publication Data
A catalogue record for this book is available from the British Library

ISBN: 9781032740027 (hbk)
ISBN: 9781032740034 (pbk)
ISBN: 9781003467175 (ebk)

DOI: 10.4324/9781003467175

Typeset in Times New Roman
by codeMantra

Contents

Acknowledgements

There are many people without whom this book would not be possible. My doctoral supervisors, Dr Peter Wright, Dr Jennifer Woodward, and Dr Andrea Wright, thank you for your guidance, encouragement, and feedback. You have always been there to offer me support and for that I am eternally grateful. I would also like to extend my gratitude to Ursula Curwen, Professor James Newman, and Dr Ewan Kirkland for their invaluable insight during various stages of this project. Likewise, I give thanks to Dr Catherine Pugh – a friend and fellow survivor of the first Theorizing Zombiism Conference – for her kind words and advice.

Dr Lara Herring, Dr Mita Lad, and Dr Martin Lewis, I am thankful to have shared my doctoral journey alongside the three of you. Your moral support has meant the world to me. Thank you for every meeting, every phone call, and every video chat. In addition, I must thank the staff of Edge Hill University's Department of Creative Arts for igniting within me a passion for academic research, as well as the staff of Liverpool Hope University for nurturing me through the completion of this book. Also, special thanks to Suzanne Richardson and Stuti Goel at Routledge for their support throughout the publishing process.

To my friend, Conor McClafferty, words cannot express my gratitude to you. Thank you for always being there for me. And to my family, thank you for your unwavering faith in me and for consistently reminding me that I can do anything I set my mind to.

Introduction

Imagine that you are playing a video game and want to explore its virtual world, which consists of a zombie-infested shopping mall. Your avatar, a 30-something photojournalist, is trying to discover the cause of the zombie outbreak. A young woman, who your avatar sees heading into a grocery store, may have answers. She will not stay in the grocery store for long, though, so you should find her quickly. However, the urgency of your avatar's situation does not matter to you right now, as you would rather sightsee. After all, the mall has an amusement park themed area with an in-door roller coaster – exciting, right? Not to mention all the shops, which have a distinct lack of security now that almost everyone in the building is dead. This being so, you take a couple of detours, directing your avatar to whack a few of those dim-witted zombies with his newly found baseball bat and try on some new clothes in the apparel shops. Granted, there are tasks to complete, but surely, there is nothing wrong with taking some time to enjoy yourself.

You spent too much time enjoying yourself. In fact, you barely considered the mysterious women despite the omnipresent signposting of your avatar's objectives on the video game interface. Time is running out to meet her, meaning you must now rush towards the grocery store. The area housing the store is under construction. Scaffolding can be seen in the distance as your avatar makes his way down a lengthy corridor. Nearly there. You dodge one lunging zombie but get grabbed by another. It takes a few seconds of your noticeably depleting time to shake the monster loose. If only every zombie in the game was like those that do not attack you: the zombies whose hands never stray from their shopping trolleys. Then, it dawns on you, as you notice one of them ahead. Those undead monsters – which call to mind both senselessness and relentless consumption – have been alluding to your behaviour. They are literal zombie consumers; you are a figurative zombie consumer.

This scenario could easily play out in Capcom's *Dead Rising* (2006). In this game, the player's avatar, Frank West, has 72 hours to uncover the truth behind a zombie outbreak in the town of Willamette, Colorado. Cases and Scoops – the game's main missions and side missions, respectively – only occur at certain times and/or under certain conditions. For instance, Case 1-1

DOI: 10.4324/9781003467175-1

is triggered at 12 p.m. during Frank's first day in Willamette. Yet, Case 1-2 will only be activated should the player complete Case 1-1 before it expires at 5 p.m. on the same day. Hence, gameplay activities in *Dead Rising* are largely determined by a timer, for which one minute equates to around 5 seconds in real time. Consequently, a sense of urgency is established by time progressing more hastily in the game's world than in our own. Should players become distracted by the allure of *Dead Rising*'s consumer-oriented setting, disastrous consequences may arise for Frank. These consequences, alongside the game's comical depictions of American people and places, ensure that *Dead Rising* is rife with what I call *videoludic satire* – that is, satire that is expressed in video games.

Satire in Video Games

Academic discourse has tended to side-step close considerations of videoludic satire. As Yi (2020) states, the domain of satirical video games has been "largely unexplored" (18) and "should be taken more seriously by practitioners and researchers" (28). This is unfortunate, as satire is hardly uncommon in video games. For instance, *BioShock Infinite* (Irrational Games, 2013), *The American Dream* (Samurai Punk, 2018), and *Night of the Consumers* (germfood, 2023) satirise American exceptionalism, gun fanaticism, and shoppers, respectively. Indeed, the presence of satire in video games is not just a contemporary phenomenon, as evidenced in Jankowski's (2022) work on satirical video games produced by politically disillusioned French developers in the mid-1980s. The reach of videoludic satire even extends to games that are not considered wholly satirical, like Konami's survival horror video game, *Silent Hill 2* (2001). In this game, players control James Sunderland: a man who travels to the titular American town of Silent Hill in search of his wife. Early in the game, James can obtain a handgun from a shopping trolley inside a derelict building. The placement of the firearm can easily be read as a satiric comment on America's lax gun laws; despite decades of mass shootings plaguing their country, Americans can still buy guns in retail outlets like Walmart.[1] Moreover, the shopping trolley's red colouration does not just make it visible against the grungy aesthetic of the building. It also suggests a conflation of consumerism and violence in the U.S.A. by alluding to the colour of blood.

Some in-game items appear more susceptible than others to be used as vessels for satiric commentary, leading to the emergence of trends regarding videoludic satire. In his examination of video game soda machines, Morrissette (2020) notes that the names of in-game commodities can carry satirical implications. For example, Sugar Water in *Halo 2: Anniversary* (Bungie, 2014) sardonically signposts the lack of nutritional value inherent in many soft drinks. Similarly, items like Nuka-Cola in Bethesda's *Fallout* series (1997 to present) can be read as satirising atomic culture: "a cultural obsession with atomic power" (Stang, 2021: 359). Certainly, the fact that Nuka-Cola bottle caps are used as currency in *Fallout* games attests to "the ways in which the series uses food products to subtly intertwine themes of toxic consumption (toxic in that it is both full of aspartame and highly irradiated), atomic culture, capitalism, and consumerism [to produce a] potent critical commentary" (Stang, 2021). Likewise, vending machines that sell items other than (or in addition to) drinks can be used to express videoludic satire. In Capcom's *Resident Evil 2* (2019), a large zombie can be seen trying to break into such a machine inside the Raccoon City Police Department. This interaction between monster and machine emphasises a latent, satirical message of the game: that zombie hunger is an extension of the gluttonous food consumption of U.S. citizens. This message is sustained throughout *Resident Evil 2* by way of its food-oriented environments. At the start of the game, the player's avatar passes through a gas station with an abundance of fast-food items; towards the end of the game, they explore a laboratory containing a cafeteria. Tellingly, the latter location is one of the most gore-laden places in *Resident Evil 2*, having been the site of a zombie feast.

The use of zombies as a metaphor for gluttons is also apparent in *Dead Rising* games, wherein the undead are explicitly compared to American citizens on the grounds that "all they do is eat."[2] Thus, recurring themes can be discerned among instances of videoludic satire. Such commonalities have been observed by Ferri (2013), whose work concentrates on the satirical video games of Molleindustria – a U.S, based, Italian game designer with a reputation for creating politically charged and controversial games. Molleindustria's portfolio of games includes *Oiligarchy* (2008): a business simulation game that foregrounds the exploitation of natural resources by the oil industry, *Phone Story* (2011): a game that dramatises and condemns the abusive processes involved in smart phone production, and *Tax Evaders* (2013): a game that centres on corporations avoiding taxes. Tying these games together are their critiques of institutional corruption and discontentment with capitalist systems of production and consumption – qualities that are also discernible in the examples of videoludic satire mentioned previously.

To fully explore and theorise videoludic satire, this book separates the phenomenon into a taxonomy comprising its distinct but potentially interrelated forms. To clarify, the forms of videoludic satire are distinct in that they are expressed in different ways, while they are potentially interrelated in that they can support one another (by having the same target, for instance). The forms of videoludic satire can be understood as *analytical lenses* (Carr, 2009: 4). In other words, they can be understood as perspectives through which researchers can study video game texts. Applying analytical lenses to video games is useful in identifying specific facets of these games for investigation. Just as "a literary theorist might focus on the use of metaphor or imagery in a text, a game scholar may choose to focus on the dynamics of reward and motivation, or the believability of the game's non-player-characters" (Bizzocchi and Tanenbaum, 2011: 305). Accordingly, the taxonomy of videoludic satire this book presents is useful to researchers aiming to produce *interpretative analyses* of video games, wherein they are read as "symbol[s] of the undercurrent of cultural and social concerns that surround [them]" (Fernández-Vara, 2019: 240).

Video games are prominent pieces of visual culture with discernible ideals, and by paying close attention to the videoludic satire expressed within them, such ideals can be brought to the forefront. This is demonstrated throughout this book via in-depth examinations of *Dead Rising* (hereafter referred to as *Dead Rising 1*) and its sequels: *Dead Rising 2* (2010), *Dead Rising 2: Off The Record* (2011), *Dead Rising 3* (2013), and *Dead Rising 4* (2016). By outlining and exploring its taxonomy of videoludic satire in relation to Capcom's zombie-based video games, this book details the capacity of videoludic satire to be communicated through the visual, auditory, and *inter(re)active* properties of video games.[3] Specifically, it addresses the aesthetic and simulated properties of gamespaces (*spatial satire*), in-game characters (*shared satire*), in-game sound (*auditory satire*), the player's temporal investments in gameplay activities (*temporal satire*), and the outcomes of in-game choices made by the player (*consequential satire*). In short, the book utilises the *Dead Rising* series to exemplify and authenticate its taxonomy, providing a detailed framework for recognising and analysing satire in video games that can be applied to games beyond those explored within its pages.

Videoludic Satire, *Dead Rising*, and (Neoliberal) Ideology

Analyses of videoludic satire can be revelatory. As King and Krzywinska (2006: 168) proclaim, video games "do not exist in a vacuum". On the contrary, they "often draw upon or produce material that has social, cultural or ideological resonances, whether these are explicit or implicit and whether they can be understood as reinforcing, negotiating or challenging meanings or assumptions generated elsewhere in society" (King and Krzywinska, 2006). Accordingly, examinations of satire in video games can help to build a picture of how these games respond to prevalent events, issues, and ideas. To revise the words of King and Krzywinska, examinations of videoludic satire can reveal what values are being reinforced, negotiated, and/or challenged in video games. Videoludic satire can thereby be indicative of a range of societal and cultural conflicts and tensions, capturing the zeitgeist of the period in which it emerges.

As is demonstrated throughout this book, applying the taxonomy of videoludic satire to the *Dead Rising* games reveals their legitimisation of hegemonic ideals, which can best be described as neoliberal. Neoliberalism is a broad term that refers to "several related economic and cultural developments [emphasising] the free market, individual entrepreneurship, private property rights, financialization, and deregulation" (Jagoda, 2020). These economic and cultural developments rose to prominence in Western societies – notably the United States of America and the United Kingdom – during the 1980s and have remained prevalent since. Primarily, then, neoliberalism describes the naturalisation of capitalism as the only valid mode of economic conduct. Consequently, the term alludes to the promotion of socio-economic competition and self-interest, as well as the permeation of these principles within social phenomena and leisure activities, like video games.

In relation to video games, neoliberalism can be understood as "an ideological background" that constitutes the promotion and glorification of ideals concerning "self-reliance and the notion that each of us is responsible for our own financial [and personal] circumstances, which we should naturally aspire to improve" (Bailes, 2019: 13.). Idealised neoliberal subjects, as constructed in video games, consist of individuals who are "free and autonomous, but also disciplined and responsible" (Oliva et al., 2016: 611). Though, it must be stressed that these characteristics must intertwine for a video game to be seen as expressing neoliberal ideals. This is because the notion of freedom is a central tenet of video games, with players often feeling like they can "act and go where they choose inside the universe of [a] game" (Muriel and Crawford, 2020: 148). Therefore, simply equating freedom in terms of player actions and choices with neoliberalism is problematic and would lead to the assumption that all video games invoke neoliberalism (Baerg, 2014: 195). Of course, this assumption is inaccurate. For example, the indie video game *Peak Bleak Blues (and other moods)* (Connor Sherlock, 2019) does not evoke neoliberal values. This game consists of several locales for the player to explore and contains no goals, no character customisation options, and no objects to be interacted with. Hence, the player's choice of where to go indicates freedom but not in a way that alludes to discipline or responsibility.

Scholarly work has emphasised the manifestation of several neoliberal values in video games, such as the ability to manage resources efficiently (Baerg, 2012; 2014; Oliva et al., 2016; Pérez-Latorre and Oliva, 2017), individualism (Baerg, 2012; Pérez-Latorre and Oliva, 2017), self-discipline (Millington, 2009), and an awareness of and capacity to manage risk (Baerg, 2012; 2014; Millington, 2009; Oliva et al., 2016). These are all discernibly neoliberal because they prioritise the notion of players being "in control of their actions and the outcomes of these actions" (Muriel and Crawford, 2020: 140). Thus, these values encourage players to aspire toward self-sufficiency in their respective gameplay contexts, whilst also framing the (potential) failings of players as the result of their own "deficiencies or lack of effort" (Muriel and Crawford, 2020: 152). In *Dead Rising* games, the neoliberal values mentioned above are legitimised by their videoludic satire, which targets excessive consumption.[4]

The Structure of the Book

Each form of videoludic satire has its own variations, which are expanded upon in subsequent chapters of this book. However, before the forms of videoludic satire can be explored, it is necessary to lay some theoretical foundations. Accordingly, Chapter 1 provides an overview of the term satire while also detailing its problematic elements. Moreover, it proposes a stipulative definition of satire; this is necessary as the term is highly contested. The chapter then highlights the connection between satire and zombies (which have long been used as vessels for socio-political commentary) before gesturing towards how this connection is maintained in video games. Finally, the chapter acknowledges existing research on satire in video games and highlights the limitations of this work – limitations that are resolved by the book's taxonomy of videoludic satire.

In Chapter 2, contextual information pertinent to satirical video games is explored, such as paratextual, thematic, and story-related material. By collecting such material in relation to the *Dead Rising* games, this chapter shows how these games recontextualise and alter the satire of George A. Romero's satirical film, *Dawn of the Dead* (1978), for post-millennial audiences. Specifically, *Dead Rising* games adopt Romero's critique of unchecked consumption to satirise the perceivably exploitative consumer rhetoric adopted by American politicians and corporations after the September 11 terrorist attacks in 2001. Additionally, they expand on the symbolic nature of undead hunger in Romero's film, in which the consumption of human flesh by zombies serves as a metaphor for U.S. citizen's drive to shop; in *Dead Rising* games, the intake of human meat by zombies also signifies human gluttony.

The critiques of excessive consumption pointed out in Chapter 2 form the basis of subsequent chapters on the forms of videoludic satire. Chapter 3 focuses on the consumption-oriented locales of *Dead Rising* games to demonstrate how spatial satire can emerge through the player's exploration of, and interaction with, video game worlds. Chapter 4 examines shared satire by focusing on zombies and non-player characters (NPCs) in *Dead Rising* games. Specifically, this chapter concentrates on how video game characters convey satire through their appearances, behaviours, and interactions with each another and the player's avatar. Chapter 5 demonstrates how auditory satire is communicated in video games via sound that plays alongside non-interactive cutscenes, accompanies player action, and signifies changes to the game state. Notably, in *Dead Rising* games, auditory satire is conveyed through sound that alludes to zombiism and consumption simultaneously. Considering the emphasis on time in *Dead Rising* games, Chapter 6 explores how the player's (mis)use of time in video games can create temporal satire. In *Dead Rising* games, this becomes apparent when players prioritise consumption-related pleasure over story-based objectives. Expanding on the previous chapter, Chapter 7 focuses on the short- and long-term outcomes of dismissing transient tasks in favour of pursuing commodities and consumables in *Dead Rising* games. As such, it argues that consequential satire occurs when choices players make during gameplay have satirical outcomes.

The conclusion of this book consolidates the previous arguments made regarding the *Dead Rising* series by drawing them together into one cohesive argument. Accordingly, it contends that *Dead Rising* games are not countercultural texts, as Romero's *Dawn of the Dead* is often believed to be. Rather, they are ideologically conservative in their legitimisation of hegemonic/neoliberal values. Moreover, the conclusion offers a speculative account of how the taxonomy of videoludic satire could be expanded. Taken together, the chapters of this book form an in-depth study on the intersections between satire and video games, establishing a taxonomy of videoludic satire that can be adopted in future investigations in this area. Furthermore, in applying its taxonomy to *Dead Rising* games, the book offers insight into the use of zombie narratives in the videoludic realm.

Notes

1 More than 20 years after the release of *Silent Hill 2*, Walmart "stopped selling AR-style firearms as well as handguns and [...] raised the age limit to purchase a firearm from 18 to 21 years old" (Woodward, 2022). Although, the retail chain does continue "to sell firearms at many of its locations" (Woodward, 2022). Therefore, the satire of *Silent Hill 2* has remained topical for decades.

2 This dialogue is stated in the first and fourth games in the series.

3 The term *inter(re)activity* was coined by Smethurst and Craps "to acknowledge the fact that during gameplay, it is not only the game that reacts to the player but also the player who reacts to the game" (2014: 273).

4 Consumption is defined in this book as "using up, destroying, or eating something" (Lehdonvitta et al., 2009: 1062).

References

Baerg, A. (2012) 'Risky Business: Neo-liberal Rationality and the Computer RPG', in Voorhees, G. A., Call, J. and Whitlock, K. (eds.) *Dungeons, Dragons, and Digital Denizens: The Digital Role-Playing Game*. New York: Bloomsbury, pp. 152–73.

Baerg, A. (2014) 'Neoliberalism, Risk, and Uncertainty in the Video Game', in Di Leo, J. R. and Mehan, U. (eds.) *Capital at the Brink: Overcoming the Destructive Legacies of Neoliberalism*. Michigan: Open Humanities Press, pp. 186–214.

Bailes, J. (2019) *Ideology and the Virtual City: Videogames, Power Fantasies, and Neoliberalism*. Winchester: Zero Books.

Bizzocchi, J. and Tanenbaum, J. (2011) 'Well Read: Applying Close Reading Techniques to Gameplay Experiences', in Davidson, D. (ed.) *Well Played 3.0: Video Games, Value and Meaning*. Pittsburgh, PA: ETC Press, pp. 289–316.

Carr, D. 2009. 'Textual Analysis, Digital Games, Zombies', *Proceedings of the 2009 DiGRA International Conference, West* London, September 1–4. Available at: https://www.digra.org/digital-library/publications/textual-analysis-digital-games-zombies/ (Accessed: 29 August 2023).

Fernández-Vara, C. (2019) *Introduction to Game Analysis*. 2nd edn. New York: Routledge.

Ferri, G. (2013) 'Rhetorics, Simulations and Games: The Ludic and Satirical Discourse of Molleindustria', *International Journal of Gaming and Computer-Mediated Simulations*, 5(1), pp. 32–49. https://doi.org/10.4018/jgcms.2013010103

Jagoda, P. (2020) 'Playing Through a Serious Crisis: On the Neoliberal Art of Video Games', *Post45*, 31 August. Available at: https://post45.org/2020/08/playing-through-a-serious-crisis-on-the-neoliberal-art-of-video-games/#footnote_7_12022

Jankowski, F. (2022) '"Sorry, You *Had* Won": Satirical French Digital Games Responding to National Sociopolitical Crisis (1984–1986)', in Bonello Rutter Giappone, K., Majkowski, T. Z. and Švelch, J. (eds.) *Video Games and Comedy*. Cham: Palgrave Macmillan, pp. 173–90.

King, G. and Krzywinska, T. (2006) *Tomb Raiders and Space Invaders: Videogame Forms and Contexts*. London: I. B. Tauris.

Lehdonvitta, V., Wilska, T.-A., and Johnson, M. (2009) 'Virtual Consumerism', *Information, Communication & Society*, 12(7), pp. 1059–79. https://doi.org/10.1080/13691180802587813

Millington, B. (2009) 'Wii Has Never Been Modern: "Active" Video Games and the "Conduct of Conduct"', *New Media & Society*, 11(4), pp. 621–40. https://doi.org/10.1177/1461444809102966

Morrissette, J. (2020) 'I'd Like to Buy the World a Nuka-Cola: The Purposes and Meanings of Video Game Soda Machines', *Game Studies: The International Journal of Computer Game Research*, 20(1). Available at: https://gamestudies.org/2001/articles/jessmorrissette (accessed 28 August 2023).

Muriel, D. and Crawford, G. (2020) 'Video Games and Agency in Contemporary Society', *Games and Culture*, 15(2), pp. 138–57. https://doi.org/10.1177/1555412017750448

Oliva, M., Pérez-Latorre, Ó. and Besalú, R. (2016) '"Choose, Collect, Manage, Win!": Neoliberalism, Enterprising Culture and Risk Society in Video Game Covers', *Convergence*, 24(6), pp. 607–22. https://doi.org/10.1177/1354856516680324

Pérez-Latorre, Ó. and Oliva, M. (2017) 'Video Games, Dystopia, and Neoliberalism: The Case of BioShock Infinite', *Games and Culture*, 14(7–8). pp. 781–800. https://doi.org/10.1177/1555412017727226

Smethurst, T. and Craps, S. (2014) 'Playing with Trauma: Interreactivity, Empathy, and Complicity in *The Walking Dead* Video Game', *Games and Culture*, 10(3), pp. 269–90. https://doi.org/10.1177/1555412014559306

Stang, S. (2021) 'Irradiated Cereal and Abject Meat: Food as Satire and Warning in the Fallout Series', *Games and Culture*, 17(3), pp. 354–73. https://doi.org/10.1177/15554120211030800

Woodward, A. 2022. 'Walmart Has Faced Calls to Ban Gun Sales for Years. Will Chesapeake Change That?', *The Independent*, 29 November. Available at: https://www.independent.co.uk/news/world/americas/crime/walmart-gun-sales-policy-firearms-b2235520.html (Accessed: 11 June 2023).

Yi, S. (2020) '"Is This a Joke?": The Delivery of Serious Content through Satirical Digital Games', *Acta Ludologica*, 3(1), pp. 18–30.

1 Satire, Zombies, Video Games

To thoroughly examine the phenomenon of videoludic satire, this book entwines several conceptual strands. Crucially, it binds notions of satire and video games: the components that make up videoludic satire. Furthermore, it takes advantage of the ties between satire and zombies: pitiful creatures with a history that doubles as an account of human anxieties. Zombie narratives can be read as receptacles for a range of cultural fears, such as the fear of enslavement, loss of selfhood, and viral contagion. Moreover, these narratives can be read as speculative explorations of societal aptitudes (or lack thereof) regarding the handling of large-scale disruptions to normative ways of life. As Bishop asserts, while initially "the zombie may appear to be a shallow and unsophisticated creature, it is instead a complex manifestation of what it means to be human" (2015: 21). Hence, as part of their multifaceted appearances across popular culture, zombie narratives have become vessels for social commentary. This, in turn, has led to their readiness to be utilised for satirical purposes.

Clarifying this book's conceptual strands, this chapter begins with an overview of satire that acknowledges the term's ambiguousness. Following this, a definition of satire is formulated. Consideration is then given to the history of the zombie, with a focus on how the creature has been appropriated for satirical purposes. Then, an account of the zombie's emergence and development within video games is provided. This account serves several purposes. It covers the practicalities of using zombies as enemies in video games, it shows how technological advancements have allowed for more complex representations of the undead in gaming, it addresses the mixed reception of videoludic zombies in academic discourse, and it situates Capcom's *Dead Rising* games within a wider landscape of culturally relevant texts. Finally, having drawn connections between satire, zombies, and video games, the chapter appraises scholarship on satire in video games. Notably, it points out the limitations of such work to justify the creation of this book's taxonomy and its subsequent application to *Dead Rising* games. To be clear, this book is not suggesting that zombies are inherently satirical, nor is it proposing that videoludic satire necessitates the presence of zombies. Rather, this book draws upon tales of

DOI: 10.4324/9781003467175-2

the undead – with their capacity for satiric expression – as a convenient way of exemplifying how videoludic satire is communicated.

Defining Satire: Complexity, Conundrum, Compromise

Satire is a multivalent concept. In fact, its etymology attests to this – deriving from the Latin phrase *lanx satura*, which can be interpreted as "a dish filled with a variety of foodstuffs" (Gilmore, 2018: 38). Yet, despite its ambiguity, researchers have made attempts to define satire. By consolidating scholarly works from the 1950s and 1960s, Griffin (1994) and Greenberg (2018) show that satire has traditionally been defined as a morally motivated – but nevertheless amusing – attack that aims to cause its target to change for the better. Likewise, Declercq argues that satire is a moralistic blend of entertainment and critique that "involves a committed effort toward resolving or alleviating [its] target's perceived social wrongness, if only by raising awareness about it" (2018: 323). However, a significant point of contention in these understandings of satire arises from their framing of satire as morally grounded.

Viewing satire as a moralising tool can be problematic. Indeed, it is easy to doubt the sincerity of canonical satirists who laud the alleged moral sentiments of their work. For instance, Jonathan Swift (1667–745) wrote that he produced his satires "with a moral View designed / To cure the Vices of Mankind," and Alexander Pope (1688–744) asserted that satire "heals with Morals what it hurts with Wit" (cited in Greenberg, 2019: 15). Yet, such proclamations may have been purely defensive. As Elkin (1973) argues, satirists active during the eighteenth century were often inclined to defend their work against critics who perceived it as little more than an exercise in sadism and spitefulness. Therefore, the promotion of satire as a moral endeavour on the part of its creators may simply be an inauthentic authorial practice. In a modern-day context, this is wryly pointed out by the satirical publication, *The Onion*, which defines satire as "the act of being a wise-ass and saying it's for a higher purpose" (cited in Greenberg, 2019: 17).

With the reformative power of satire in dispute, researchers have suggested alternative purposes for satire. For example, Griffin (1994) asserts that satire can be "an exploratory attempt to arrive at truth" (52), "a critique of false understanding" (52), an attempt "to win the admiration and applause of a reading audience [...] for the brilliant wit and force of the satirist as rhetorician" (71), or an activity in which the satirist is able to "indulge in [their] imagination's power to create" (94). Griffin's third purpose of satire is also reinforced by Diehl's admission that satire often "sacrifices the quality of moral arguments in order to meet the requirement of displaying wit or entertaining the audience" (2013: 312). Importantly, the aforesaid purposes of satire imply that the phenomenon is more likely to entertain, intrigue, or even spite its audiences than alter their actions or ignite within them sparks of revolutionary upheaval.

It is likely due to the ease in which traditional notions of satire can be destabilised that Greenberg points out a tendency among researchers to "put the definitional questions [of satire] to one side" (2019: 12) in favour of commencing with analyses of satirical texts. Still, a recurring strategy in modern scholarship involves conceptualising satire based on the shared features of said texts. For instance, Hume (2007) proposes nine features that are common in satirical works: a targeted attack, humour or wit, a sense of haughtiness on the part of the author, elements of distortion or fantasy, the acknowledgement of a moral/existential truth, authorial indignation, a purpose to inquire other than outright condemn, a clear moral standard, and a reformative aim. Likewise, Condren endorses a recognition of satire "by virtue of a contingent range of characteristics" (2012: 386) pertaining to its purposes (moral criticism, amusement, group consolidation) and communicative techniques (ridicule, irony, and humour). Cluster accounts of satire come with their own difficulties, though. For one, the exact number of features required to distinguish satire is prone to debate. In fact, Hume remarks that "one could doubtless add other features" (2007: 306) to her cluster account of satire. Furthermore, as pointed out by Declercq (2018: 320), the proposed familiarities of satire may eventually broaden to the point of all-inclusiveness, undermining the concept entirely. If everything can be considered satire, the term becomes meaningless.

The key dilemma in defining satire is as follows. Essentialist definitions of satire are easily destabilised, leading to wider understandings of the concept based on the shared characteristics of satirical works. Inevitably, these updated understandings of satire become too expansive, resulting in the need for more discriminatory definitions of satire. Such a cyclical process accomplishes little more than an endless back-and-forth in scholarly debate: a cycle I do not wish to partake in. Accordingly, by recognising that it is more fruitful for researchers to construct stipulative definitions of satire to contextualise the concept in relation to their own work, the definition of satire I adopt in this book is as follows. Satire is a targeted attack (on a specific person, group, institution, or practice) that is communicated in an entertaining manner.

Regarding the above definition of satire, satiric attacks might involve denouncing the alleged immorality of their targets and, as a result, indicate attempts by satirists to amend the behaviour of others. In this sense, prior understandings of satire are retained. However, it must be acknowledged that satiric attacks cannot *exclusively* be envisioned as moralising tools. Certainly, attacks of satire can condemn many discernible flaws and personal shortcomings that might not be considered immoral, such as "ugliness, clumsiness, foolishness, bad taste, [and] stupidity" (Knight, 2004: 5). Hence, while the moralising attempts of satirists may be discernible within works of satire, the definition of satire I present in this book does not consider them essential to its attacks. Furthermore, the "entertaining manner" by which satire is expressed does *not* allude to the medium through which satire is communicated.

Otherwise, any criticism expressed by a video game could be interpreted as satire by default since video games are a popular form of entertainment. Instead, the entertaining manner by which satire is expressed refers to the tried and tested techniques of satire. Arguably, the most recognisable of these techniques are wit or humour, though additional techniques include parody, exaggeration, allegory, grotesquery, caricature, and irony.

Any potential for the attacks of satire to trigger societal change is not assumed in this book's definition of satire. Moreover, it would be incorrect to assume that works of satire always aim to be transformative. On the contrary, such works may be more concerned with impressing or amusing audiences than encouraging individual or societal change. Attacks of satire might also function less as calls for change and more as figurative "safety valve[s]" that allow for "dissatisfaction with an existing state of affairs to dissipate itself harmlessly" (Gilmore, 2018: 184–5). This is particularly true of videoludic satire in *Dead Rising* games, which, as is demonstrated throughout this book, enforces rather than challenges hegemonic values. This is not to say that such satiric attacks lack importance, though, as they can be indicative of cultural tensions and pressure points, nonetheless. Accordingly, just as horror media can be viewed as vessels through which dominant fears and anxieties can be explored and interrogated, satire can be seen as a means of rejecting and reinforcing certain ideas and behaviours.

Satire and Zombies

Zombie narratives are meaningful; they can be read as metaphors that explore a range of socio-political issues and horrifying phenomena whilst centralising the deterioration of human agency as their core concern. As a mutable signifier, the zombie has a rich history that encompasses a trio of overlapping periods: "taking in African tribal mythology, its relocation and reanimation in the Caribbean in the African diaspora, and its final shift into mediation and the cinema" (May, 2022: 33). It is beyond the scope of this book to cover this history in depth. Besides, this gargantuan task has already been tackled in Bishop's *American Zombie Gothic* (2010) and Luckhurst's *Zombies: A Cultural History* (2015). However, consideration of the zombie's transition from folklore to film is essential in exploring the creature's subsequent relationship with satire.

The first zombie films were produced in the United States of America. These films modelled their undead on the "Dead Men Working in the Cane Fields [of Haiti]," as described in the sensationalist travel writing of William Seabrook in *The Magic Island* (1929). According to Seabrook, a zombie "is a soulless human corpse, still dead, but taken from the grave and endowed by sorcery with a mechanical semblance of life [typically for the purpose of servitude]" (1929: 93). Films like *White Zombie* (1932) utilised the figure of the zombie to channel imperialist anxieties relating to "slave uprisings and reverse colonisation" (Bishop, 2010: 13). That is to say, the horror of early zombie cinema did not stem from the liminality of zombies themselves as living-dead beings. Rather, it stemmed from the transition of this pitiful state of existence from black to white individuals – a transition that was often depicted with the zombification of a white woman. Furthermore, parallels can also be drawn between the subjugated undead of 1930s and 1940s zombie films and the disenfranchised proletariat during the Great Depression (1929–39); see Dendle (2007: 46), Russell (2014: 23), and Bishop (2015: 8), all of whom liken the monotonous lumbering of early zombie cinema's undead workers to that of Americans awaiting nourishment in Depression-era breadlines. Evidently, in an imperial, patriarchal, or economic sense, zombie films have dramatised human exploitation and marginalisation.

During the mid-twentieth century, Cold War fears of communist infiltration gave rise to films like *Teenage Zombies* (1959). In this film, the villainous Dr. Myra (Katherine Victor) works under "orders from the East" to enslave Americans by developing and spreading a zombifying chemical compound. Notwithstanding its campy tone, *Teenage Zombies* arguably channelled anxieties of brainwashing during America's Red Scare. Other zombie films of the period evoked fears of invasion even more fantastically, alongside fears of nuclear Armageddon. This is apparent in a duo of films featuring alien assailants: *Plan 9 from Outer Space* (1959) and *Invisible Invaders* (1959). In both films, extra-terrestrials reanimate human corpses to serve as undead soldiers in their respective assaults against humanity, which they fear has become too powerful for its own good. For Russell, the fixation of these films on mass death explicates "the realities of a nuclear war: a mountain of corpses" (2014: 51). Significantly, these films convey an emerging development in zombie cinema from merely reproducing societal angsts towards engaging in critical commentary.

In 1968, George A. Romero effectively revolutionised the zombie with the release of *Night of the Living Dead*. Stripping the zombie of its ties to a puppet master, Romero re-established this pitiful being as an autonomous, infectious, and cannibalistic monster. Moreover, it was not just the fundamentals of the zombie's existence that Romero altered. Despite the cultural and historical significance of zombie films preceding Romero's, it was his that imbued the undead with overt socio-political commentary (Wetmore Jr., 2011: 12). Likewise, *Night of the Living Dead* marks the inception of the overtly satirical zombie narrative due to its exposé of "the profound fragmentation in social structures" (Wells, 2000: 82). The film evokes imagery of societal meltdown, with its depictions of rampant militia and bleak news coverage that resonated strongly with Vietnam War era America. Yet, it is perhaps the assaults on familial units that are expressed most spectacularly in *Night of the Living Dead* – particularly in the film's violent portrayal of a child-turned-zombie cannibalising her father and bludgeoning her mother to death.

Night of the Living Dead may be considered the prototypical satirical zombie film, but its sequel, *Dawn of the Dead*, is the true forerunner of satirical zombie narratives. In fact, to fully comprehend the satire of *Dead Rising* games, it is necessary to understand the satire of this film, which is widely accepted as a critique of American capitalism and consumerism (Loudermilk, 2003; Bishop, 2010; Wetmore, Jr., 2011; Russell, 2014; Luckhurst, 2015). *Dawn of the Dead* centres on the struggles of Francine "Fran" (Gaylen Ross), Stephen (David Emge), Roger (Scott Reiniger), and Peter (Ken Foree) as they seek refuge in a zombie-infested United States. Eventually, the quartet find their way to a shopping mall: a glaring symbol of American Capitalist consumption. Here, they settle and attempt to preserve a sense of *bourgeois* normality: "they play games of makeup, acting out the roles of elegance and wealth (and the attendant stereotypes of gender, class, and race) that they dreamed of, but weren't able actually to afford, in their previous middle-class lives" (Shaviro, 1993: 92). This proves to be fruitless when the mall, initially considered a fortress and utopia, is proven to be physically and conceptually vulnerable when zombies overtake the structure.

Dawn of the Dead satirises "the false security of consumer society" (Loudermilk, 2003: 90). In other words, it satirises the notion that consumerism can solve any problem. The film's satire is expressed directly when Roger and Stephen die while prioritising the ownership of material goods over their own safety. Roger dies after he is bitten by a zombie as he tries to retrieve a bag of tools he dropped outside the mall (even though he could doubtlessly have attained more tools inside building), whereas Stephen dies after he is assaulted by several zombies while refusing to abandon the mall after it is raided by a biker gang. In each instance, when the pair transform into zombies, the film strengthens a key component of its satire: the insinuation that zombie hunger is symbolic of, and satirical of, consumer greed. This insinuation is also communicated in Stephen's musings on why the undead want to occupy the mall. It was "an important place" in their previous lives, he presumes, thereby inferring that zombies are drawn to the mall by their consumption-oriented, residual memories. *Dawn of the Dead* can therefore be read as a "cautionary tale for consumer America" (Loudermilk, 2003: 85). Indeed, Fran and Peter survive the events of the film because they resist the pull of consumer items instead of being fatally hypnotised by them, escaping the mall by helicopter.

Since the release of *Dawn of the Dead*, the zombie-as-consumer (and the consumer-as-zombie) has become a persistent image in American popular culture and beyond. As Loudermilk asserts, Romero's film has become "a tale disseminated, an allegory mutated, an anti-commodity serially re-commodified into an ideological trend" (2003: 98). The cinematic undead have proceeded to assault the living inside malls in the remake of *Dawn of the Dead* (2004), *Land of the Dead* (2005), and *Maze Runner: The Scorch Trials* (2015), as well as in video games like *Stubbs the Zombie in Rebel Without a Pulse* (2005) and *Left 4 Dead 2* (2009). Furthermore, beyond evoking the consumption of material goods, zombies have been used as satirical stand-ins for consumers of television. In "Treehouse of Horror III," a Halloween special of the long running animated sitcom *The Simpsons* (1989 to present), the titular family return to their couch after evading the undead and, with vacant expressions, ironically remark that "at least [they're] not zombies" (cited in Loudermilk, 2003: 97). Several years later, Charlie Brooker's *Dead Set* (2008) would feature zombies staring obsessively at screens broadcasting live footage from the reality television programme, *Big Brother* (2000 to present).

Satirical jabs at ravenous food consumption are also ostensible in zombie fiction, as touched on in the introduction of this book. Likewise, *The Simpsons* again draws on zombiism to parody consumers in "Treehouse of Horror XX," wherein a newly formulated burger transforms Springfield's citizens into cannibalistic killers called "munchers." Clearly, the zombie consumer has become a recurring image in popular culture, always "leaving at least the residue of *Dawn*'s critique of the false security of consumer society" (Loudermilk, 2003: 97–8). Therefore, while it may be assumed that "[the zombie] is, above all, a creature designed to induce terror" (May, 2022: 37), it should equally be recognised as a monster that is inclined to provoke feelings of pity, dark humour, criticism, self-reflection, and satire.

Zombies and Video Games

Despite the allegorical depth of zombies in film, zombies in video games are often viewed as devoid of meaning. Attesting to this, early games featuring zombies had rudimentary visuals, narrative backdrops, and gameplay mechanics. Arguably, the first game to feature zombies was the Atari 2600's *Entombed* (1982), in which the player moves their avatar through a maze that constantly rises towards the top of the screen. If the player's avatar is pushed off the screen or touches one of the zombies that occupy the maze, they will die. Yet, the game's antagonists are only perceivable as zombies due to the brief narrative exposition on the back of boxes for *Entombed*. Here, it is stated that a team of archaeologists stumbled into the "catacombs of the zombies" – although the so-called zombies have as much detail as stick figures and thus leave much to the imagination. Confusing matters further, box art for *Entombed* features an archaeologist being attacked by a ghost.

Like *Entombed*, many early video games featuring zombies used basic character models due to technical limitations: see *Zombies* (1983) (also known as *Realm of Impossibility*) and *Zombie Zombie* (1984), which released for the Atari 8-bit family and the ZX Spectrum, respectively. Surpassing these games visually, others like *Ghosts 'n Goblins* (1985) for arcade machines, *Horror Zombies from the Crypt* (1990) for the PC, and Zombies Ate My Neighbors (1993) for the SNES depicted the undead with more detail. Functionally, though, there is nothing separating their zombies from the plethora of other creatures featured within these games. Be it zombies, werewolves, vampires, or even giant babies, all are just the "bad guys" – enemies that fit neatly into simple binaries of good avatars versus evil monsters. However, Capcom's

Resident Evil (1996), which saw zombies rendered in three dimensions on Sony's PlayStation, altered this binary somewhat with narrative information (notes and diary entries are scattered throughout this game's mansion setting). Most famously, the "Keeper's Diary" charts the physical and mental deterioration of a man transforming into a zombie over several days. Thus, alongside the game's attribution of zombiism to corporate greed (its zombies originate from a pharmaceutical company's covert creation of bioweapons), *Resident Evil* humanised the undead in a way that was unprecedented in video games at the time of its release.

Zombie video games have been credited with "incubating" (Bishop, 2010: 16) the zombie genre during its decline in popularity from the 1990s until its post-millennial resurgence, which began with two blockbuster films: Danny Boyle's *28 Days Later* (2002) and Paul W.S. Anderson's *Resident Evil* (2002). Yet, video game developers did not simply hand over the proverbial baton to filmmakers after the turn of the century. Instead, they continued to produce zombie video games and video games featuring zombies at a rapid pace. Capcom continued making *Resident Evil* games, resulting in eight numbered titles and multiple spin-offs, remakes, and re-imaginings over the decades since the first game's release. In addition, zombies and zombie-like creatures featured prominently in more recent video game series, such as *Dead Rising* (2006 to present), *Left 4 Dead* (2008–2009), *Dead Island* (2011–2023), *State of Decay* (2013 to present), *The Last of Us* (2013–2022), *Dying Light* (2015–2022), and *Arizona Sunshine* (2016–2023). Even the bright and cheerful *Super Mario Odyssey* (2017) lets players make Mario appear undead with an unlockable zombie outfit.

The ubiquity of zombies in video games has been accredited to a variety of reasons. For instance, it has been said that zombies are "economical in terms of storytelling" (Leinfellner, cited in Barr, 2020: 18). That is, they do not require detailed narrative exposition as players are primed to know what they are given their prevalence in popular culture. Moreover, the presence of zombies in video games justifies the inclusion of correspondingly fantastical settings: typically, post-apocalyptic environments. Also, video game zombies can be cost-effective compared to other enemy types, as they "require only rudimentary [artificial intelligence] to implement" (Barr, 2020: 21). Yet, the most cited reason for the popularity of zombies in video games is their convenience as morally uncompromising cannon fodder. As Krzywinska asserts, zombies serve as "perfect enemies that can be killed without incurring guilt in the name of survival" (2008: 168) – a sentiment that has been echoed over the years by scholars like Hunt (2015: 115), Perron (2020: 209), and Wintle (2023: 10). The attention given to the bodily destruction of the undead in video games is not unwarranted, as many video games featuring zombies are incredibly violent. However, this fixation can result in scholars making generalisations about zombie video games and zombies in video games. Namely, that the digital dead are "devoid of much deep psychological, aesthetic, or political meaning" (Krzywinska, 2008: 165).

A key question regarding zombies in video games is posited by Backe and Aarseth (2013: 13), who consider whether the "ludification" of the undead neutralises their allegorical potential, or whether it can be beneficial to it. Leaning towards the latter, Weise (2009; 2011) posits that *Dead Rising 1* problematises consumerism and, by extension, Western capitalist principles in his work on procedural adaptations. Modelled after Bogost's (2007) concept of procedural rhetoric, which describes the ability of videogames to express arguments via their rule-based systems, procedural adaptation describes instances wherein video games take recognisable elements from other (non-gaming) media texts and presents these elements through their visual and ludic properties. To exemplify this, Weise (2009) contends that *Dead Rising 1* is a procedural adaptation of *Dawn of the Dead*, meaning that "the situations of [Romero's] film, and the complex logic they imply, [serve as] the naked blueprint for [this game]" (2009: 260). However, while Weise forthrightly claims that *Dead Rising 1* offers "a sharp satirical view of America in the tradition of classic zombie cinema [and, specifically, Romero's oeuvre]" (2011: 166), the precise nature of the game's satire remains largely unexplored in his work. Instead, Weise focuses on "the behaviours of the zombie itself, and the dynamics of dwindling safety which are the common dilemma of zombie film protagonists" (2009: 252).

Aside from focusing on the visceral and behavioural qualities of the undead in video games, researchers have begun to recognise the potential of the videoludic zombie in recent years – aligning it more with its other popular cultural depictions, which can be viewed as "perfect *tabula rasa*[*s*] upon which one can project any symbolic, metaphoric, or allegorical meaning" (Knickerbocker, 2015: 72). Accordingly, researchers have asserted that video game zombies can manifest "potential fears and anxieties concerning mortality, infection, and the natural environment itself" (Bishop, 2015: 147) alongside "modern medical fears" like biohazards (Fawcett and McGreevy, 2020: 96). Zombie video games have also been identified as sites for interrogating the politics of race (Brock, 2011) and gender (Nae, 2022). Yet, despite the longstanding relationship between satire and zombies in popular culture, its videoludic manifestations have only been touched upon lightly. Thus, when Schott writes of *Dead Rising 1*'s adoption of satirical elements from Romero's *Dawn of the Dead*, he illuminates this predominantly with reference to a single cutscene in which a store owner "laments the death of consumerism over and above his own demise" (2011: 150). As such, there is room for more focused examinations of the cross-sections between zombies, satire, and video games that incorporate the visual and inter(re)active components of these games.

Theorising Videoludic Satire

As the introduction of this book has shown, satire in video games is hardly uncommon. Yet, the same cannot be said of theorisations of videoludic satire in academic scholarship. Ferri even stresses "the need for further research [on satire in games]" (2013: 47), calling for the development of descriptive terms and research methodologies to better understand satire in games. This call has remained unanswered, though some research does lead towards fulfilling Ferri's appeal. For example, Schellekens et al. (2020) reconceptualise a taxonomy of game components proposed by Treanor et al. (2011) to produce a broad framework for game designers to foreground their satirical intent. However, this is not accomplished unproblematically.

Schellekens et al. argue that satire can be expressed by a game's *operational elements* (such as in-game characters and game mechanics) and its *interpreted components* (such as themes and aesthetics). Yet, while the differentiation of video game components put forward by Treanor et al. may be useful in conceptualising games as discrete but interrelated meaning-making units, it does not lend itself well to categorising the ways in which videoludic satire can be expressed. This is because operational elements in isolation do not provide enough information on a game's satiric intent and must thereby "interact with interpreted components [...] to convey [this]" (Schellekens et al., 2020). As Kirkland asserts, meaning in video games "can be seen as located in the intersection between audiovisual design, gameplay, and context" (2009: 164). So, in separating these elements, Schellekens et al. inevitably fragment the meaning of video game texts. This means that, despite aiming to address the satiric potential of Treanor et al.'s video game components separately, Schellekens et al. must continuously cross-reference between these components for their analyses of videoludic satire to make sense. Therefore, the latter do not propose secure categories for the analysis of videoludic satire.

Perhaps the most substantial attempt at theorising satire in video games comes from Wilcox (2013), who coined the term *ludic satire* to describe the process by which games can "[critique] *elected* performance, action, or choice" (n.p.) and thereby transform their players into objects of satire. To explain his concept, Wilcox draws heavily upon two video games that appear critical of virtual violence: *Metal Gear Solid 3: Snake Eater* (Konami, 2004) (hereafter referred to as *MGS3*) and *Grand Theft Auto IV* (Rockstar Games, 2008) (hereafter referred to as *GTA IV*). The first of these games focuses on a commando as he attempts to prevent the use of weapons of mass destruction, while the second tells the story of an Eastern European war veteran whose pursuit of the "American Dream" goes awry.

According to Wilcox, only *MGS3* produces ludic satire. This is because players are given the choice to either partake in or avoid lethal combat in this game. Thus, violence in *MGS3* is not compulsory. It only occurs if the player chooses to pursue deadly acts of aggression. As explained by Wilcox, ludic satire can emerge during a late stage of *MGS3*, in which the player's avatar is confronted by the ghosts of the enemies he has killed while traversing a riverbed. For Wilcox, the spectral re-appearances of enemies that the avatar has slain serves as a reminder to trigger-happy players that they could have tranquilised, or otherwise avoided, these enemies. Therefore, the trajectories in *MGS3* that stem from the player's decision to either murder or sedate the game's enemies (and consequently traverse the riverbed in a guilt-ridden or guilt-free fashion) are what enables ludic satire to manifest. In contrast, Wilcox asserts that *GTA IV* does not show evidence of ludic satire because its violence is inescapable; *GTA IV* does not include choice elements that would free its avatar from a life of crime. Hence, while *GTA IV* may encourage players to question whether they are comfortable simulating barbarous actions (Sicart, 2011: 105), Wilcox claims that "the game cannot both satirize the player while maintaining that character is fate" (2013: n.p.). In other words, Wilcox argues that *GTA IV* may be read on a purely narrative level as a satire on the construction of video games as characteristically violent pastimes, but not as a satirisation of players who partake in the violence that the game demands.

Wilcox's ludic satire points to a distinctive affordance of video games: the ability to enable their players to make meaningful choices that have significant repercussions within their worlds. Yet, in doing so, it overlooks satire in video games that arises from non-negotiable sequences of gameplay. Given Wilcox's definition of ludic – as "[o]f or relating to playfulness" (2013: n.p.)[1] – this satire should also fall under the umbrella of ludic satire. As such, even if *GTA IV* expresses satire on violent video games in general, rather than the player's engagement in such games, this satire still emerges through gameplay. In other words, it is still ludic. Furthermore, and perhaps more significantly, video games can successfully satirise their players through means other than in-game choices. For instance, *Phone Story* consists of four linear gameplay scenarios that do this.

Released for the iPhone before being banned by Apple and subsequently re-released as an internet browser game, *Phone Story* initially aimed to "provoke a critical reflection on its own technological platform" (Phone Story, 2011). Each of the game's scenarios was designed to utilise the iPhone's touchscreen. In the first scenario, players take control of two soldiers in the Democratic Republic of the Congo who are guarding a group of enslaved children. The children are mining for coltan: an ore containing minerals used in the production of smartphones. The goal is to sustain their exploitation by tapping on children who stop working. When a child is tapped, one of the soldiers will approach the child and point their gun at them in an act of intimidation that makes the child resume working. In the second scenario, the location shifts to a factory in China where the player is tasked with preventing the deaths of unhappy workers who throw themselves from the top of the building. This is done by dragging a "suicide prevention net" across the bottom of the screen. The third scenario, which is set in a non-descript Western setting, has the player controlling a shop assistant who must throw smartphones at approaching customers. Finally, in the fourth scenario, the player needs to differentiate between various types of waste (from discarded smartphone products) by dragging them from a conveyor belt to a worker in another non-descript but discernibly non-Western locale. After this, the entire process begins again.

Purchasers of Apple's iPhone products (originally the game's assumed players) are clearly satirised on the grounds of their complicity in the cycle that *Phone Story* dramatises. As argued by Ferri (2013), this satire is achieved as gameplay in *Phone Story* transforms the players' indirect involvement with what it presents as Apple's unethical practices into direct involvement within the world of the game. Hence, *Phone Story* successfully satirises its players without providing them with a series of in-game choices that have varying consequences. Furthermore, when players of satirical games are confronted with in-game choices, the outcomes of these choices are not always constructed with the intent of satirising players directly. As Ferri's examination of *Oiligarchy* shows, satirical games may incorporate in-game choices as a means of satirising other targets. In this game, the player takes on the role of a Western oil-extraction corporation CEO who is tasked with generating capital above all else. This goal eventually proves to be unmaintainable and can lead to dire consequences, like nuclear war (Ferri, 2013: 39).

Players can make different choices regarding their gameplay style in *Oiligarchy*. They can choose to ruthlessly exploit the earth, which leads to its destruction, or they can choose to mitigate such exploitation, which eventually sees human civilisation transcend its reliance on fossil fuels to achieve an eco-friendly existence. Such in-game choices present positive and negative outcomes. Hence, *Oiligarchy* manifests ludic satire according to Wilcox's definition of the term, as the game provides the player with "the *option* to become the object of derision [in this case, a greedy CEO] and then demonstrate[s] the folly of that *choice* [by depicting a scenario wherein the world ends]" (2013: n.p.). Although, as Ferri (2013) asserts, *Oiligarchy* aims to make people aware of the problematics of oil extraction. Hence, instead of blaming players for the systematic imperfections of oil retrieval, the game utilises choice-based gameplay to satirise corporate bodies that care more about making money than societal and ecological welfare. Ergo, *Oiligarchy* makes it clear that video games can conform to the specificities of Wilcox's ludic satire whilst satirising targets other than their players.

Clearly, videoludic satire can manifest in varying ways. It can arise from in-game decisions that players of non-linear games make to transform them into objects of satire, and it can be achieved in linear games through enforced gameplay activities. Moreover, even when in-game choices are included in satirical games, these choices cannot be said to satirise players of these games exclusively. Adding to this, in both linear and non-linear games, videoludic satire can be encountered by players via environmental exploration – this enables players to encounter a plethora of in-game locations, items, characters, sounds, and activities that are filled with satiric potential. Accordingly, this book presents an original taxonomy of videoludic satire comprising several terms to describe its varied manifestations: spatial satire, shared satire, auditory satire, temporal satire, and consequential satire. Taken collectively, these terms allow for the full scope of videoludic satire to be explored. Moreover, the terms proposed in this book do not classify videoludic satire arbitrarily. Rather, they consider the overarching ways in which videoludic satire can be expressed by means of the representational, simulated, and inter(re)active aspects of video games.

Note

1 This definition appears in an image at the top of Wilcox's essay, which shows the dictionary definition of the word ludic.

References

Backe, H-J and Aarseth, E. (2013) 'Ludic Zombies: An Examination of Zombieism in Games', *Proceedings of the 2013 DiGRA International Conference: DeFragging Game Studies*. Available at: https://www.digra.org/digital-library/publications/ludic-zombies-an-examination-of-zombieism-in-games/ (Accessed: 01 December 2023).

Barr, M. (2020) 'Zombies, Again? A Qualitative Analysis of the Zombie Antagonist's Appeal in Game Design', in Webley S. J. and Zackariasson P. (eds.) *The Playful Undead and Video Games: Critical Analyses of Zombies and Gameplay*. New York, Routledge, pp. 15–29.

Bishop, K. W. (2010) *American Zombie Gothic: The Rise and Fall (and Rise) of the Walking Dead in Popular Culture*. Jefferson, NC: McFarland.

Bishop, K. W. (2015) *How Zombies Conquered Popular Culture: The Multifarious Walking Dead in the 21st Century*. Jefferson, NC: McFarland.

Bogost, I. (2007) *Persuasive* Games*: The Expressive Power of Videogames*. Cambridge, MA: MIT Press.

Brock, A. (2011) '"When Keeping it Real Goes Wrong": Resident Evil 5, Racial Representation, and Gamers', *Games and Culture*, 6(5), pp. 429–52. https://doi.org/10.1177/1555412011402676

Condren, C. (2012) 'Satire and Definition', *Humor: International Journal of Humor Research*, 25(4), pp. 375–99. https://doi.org/10.1515/humor-2012-0019

Declercq, D. (2018) 'A Definition of Satire (And Why a Definition Matters', *The Journal of Aesthetics and Art Criticism*, 76(3), pp. 319–30. https://doi.org/10.1111/jaac.12563

Dendle, P. (2007) 'The Zombie as Barometer of Cultural Anxiety', in Scott, N. (ed.) *Monsters and the Monstrous: Myths and Metaphors of Enduring Evil*. Amsterdam: Rodopi, pp. 45–57.

Elkin, P. K. (1973) *The Augustan Defence of Satire*. Oxford: Clarendon Press.

Fawcett, C. and McGreevy, A. (2020) 'Resident Evil and Infections Fear', in Webley S. J. and Zackariasson P. (eds.) *The Playful Undead and Video Games: Critical Analyses of Zombies and Gameplay*. New York, Routledge, pp. 85–98.

Ferri, G. (2013) 'Rhetorics, Simulations and Games: The Ludic and Satirical Discourse of Molleindustria', *International Journal of Gaming and Computer-Mediated* Simulations, 5(1), pp. 32–49. https://doi.org/10.4018/jgcms.2013010103

Gilmore, J. T. (2018) *Satire*. New York: Routledge.

Greenberg, J. (2019) *The Cambridge Introduction to Satire*. Cambridge: Cambridge University Press.

Griffin, D. (1994) *Satire: A Critical Reintroduction*. Lexington: University Press of Kentucky.

Hume, K. (2007) 'Diffused Satire in Contemporary American Fiction', *Modern* Philology, 105(2), pp. 300–25. https://doi.org/10.1086/588102

Hunt, N. (2015) 'A Utilitarian Antagonist: The Zombie in Popular Video Games', in Hubner, L., Leaning, M. and Manning, P. (eds.) *The Zombie Renaissance in* Popular *Culture*. Basingstoke: Palgrave Macmillan, pp. 107–23.

Kirkland, E. (2009) 'Masculinity in Video Games: The Gendered Gameplay of Silent Hill', *Camera Obscura*, 24(2[71]), pp. 161–83. https://doi.org/10.1215/02705346-2009-006

Knickerbocker, D. (2015) 'Why Zombies Matter: The Undead as Critical Posthumanist', *Bohemic Litteraria*, 18(2), pp. 59–82. Available at: https://hdl.handle.net/11222.digilib/135003 (Accessed: 01 December 2023).

Knight, C. A. 2004. *The Literature of Satire*. Cambridge: Cambridge University Press.

Krzywinska, T. (2008) 'Zombies in Gamespace: Form, Context, and Meaning in Zombie-Based Video Games', in McIntosh, S. and Leverette, M. (eds.) *Zombie Culture: Autopsies of the Living Dead*. Lanham, MD: Scarecrow Press, Inc., pp. 153–68.

Loudermilk, A. (2003) 'Eating 'Dawn' in the Dark: Zombie Desire and Commodified Identity in George A. Romero's 'Dawn of the Dead'', *Journal of Consumer* Culture, 3(1), pp. 83–108. https://doi.org/10.1177/1469540503003001228

Luckhurst, R. (2015) *Zombies: A Cultural History*. London: Reaktion Books.

May, L. (2022) *Digital Zombies, Undead Stories: Narrative Emergence and Videogames*. New York: Bloomsbury.

Nae, A. (2022) *Immersion, Narrative, and Gender Crisis in Survival Horror Video Games*. New York: Routledge.

Perron, B. (2020) 'The Pace and Reach of Video Game Zombies', in Webley S. J. and Zackariasson P. (eds.) *The Playful Undead and Video Games: Critical Analyses of Zombies and Gameplay*. New York: Routledge, pp. 197–215.

Phone Story (2011) *Phone Story*. Available at: https://www.phonestory.org/ (Accessed: 01 December 2023)

Russell, J. 2014. *Book Of The Dead: The Complete History Of Zombie Cinema*. London: Titan Books.

Schellekens, J., Caselli, S., Gualeni, S. and Bonello Rutter Giappone, K. (2020) 'Satirical Game Design: The Case of the Boardgame Construction BOOM!', in *Proceedings of the 15th International Conference on the Foundations of Digital Games*. https://doi.org/10.1145/3402942.3403008

Schott, G. (2011) 'Digital Dead: Translating the Visceral and Satirical Elements of George A. Romero's Dawn of the Dead to Videogames', in Moreman, C. M. and Rushton, C. J. (eds.) *Zombies* Are *Us: Essays on the Humanity of the Walking Dead*. Jefferson, NC: McFarland, pp. 141–50.

Seabrook, W. (1929) *The Magic Island*. Reprint 2016. New York: Dover Publications, Inc.

Shaviro, S. (1993) *The Cinematic Body*. Minneapolis: University of Minnesota Press.

Sicart, M. (2011) *The Ethics of Computer Games*. Cambridge, MA: MIT Press.

Treanor, M. et al., (2011) 'Proceduralist readings: how to find meaning in games with graphical logics', *Proceedings of the 6th International Conference on Foundations of Digital Games*. https://doi.org/10.1145/2159365.2159381

Weise, M. (2009) 'The Rules of Horror: Procedural Adaptation in Clock Tower, Resident Evil, and Dead Rising', in Perron, B. (ed.) *Horror Video Games: Essays on the Fusion of Fear and Play*. Jefferson, NC: McFarland, pp. 238–66.

Weise, M. J. (2011) 'How the Zombie Changed Videogames', in Moreman, C. M. and Rushton, C. J. (eds.) *Zombies Are Us: Essays on the Humanity of the Walking* Dead. Jefferson, NC: McFarland, pp. 151–68.

Wells, P. (2000) *The Horror Genre: From Beelzebub to Blair Witch*. London: Wallflower Press.

Wetmore, Jr. and K. J. (2011) *Back from the Dead: Remakes of the Romero Zombie Films as Markers of Their Times*. Jefferson, NC: McFarland.

Wilcox, S. (2013) 'From Monopoly to Metal Gear: A Survey of Ludic Satire', First *Person Scholar*, 25 September. Available at: https://www.firstpersonscholar.com/from-monopoly-to-metal-gear/ (Accessed: 01 December 2023).

Wintle, P. (2023) 'Mutants and Zombies Everywhere! Or Villains, Violence, and Selfishness: Questions of Humanity in the Post-Apocalyptic (Pandemic) Video Game', *Games and Culture*, pp. 1–22. https://doi.org/10.1177/15554120231182802

2 Contextualising Videoludic Satire

To understand the videoludic satire of Capcom's *Dead Rising* series – as with any other satirical video game or gaming franchise – knowledge of the zeitgeist in which it emerged is crucial. This is because satire is ephemeral. In other words, it is bound to cultural and temporal perceptions, which are subject to change. Therefore, contextual information pertinent to satirical games must be foregrounded so that the satire they express can be understood. Accordingly, in this chapter, paratextual, thematic, and story-related material and information relative to *Dead Rising* games is considered to determine what these games satirise and how they convey contemporaneousness. Furthermore, to aid in the contextualisation of videoludic satire in these games, Fernández-Vara's (2019) comprehensive list of investigative areas for video game studies is utilised. For Fernández-Vara, knowledge of a game's production team, genre, technological platform, socio-historical context, marketisation, target audience, relations to other media, fictional world, and story may all prove useful to video game researchers. Certainly, these areas can strengthen one's understanding of videoludic satire, though not all of them need to be addressed for this purpose. Researchers can be selective with the areas they elect to pursue in contextualising videoludic satire. Some may be fruitful while others may not, as is the case when unpacking the satire of *Dead Rising* games.

The first section of this chapter explains what *Dead Rising* games satirise and provides a concise overview of their story elements, which are expanded upon in subsequent sections. The second section then claims that understanding the satire of George A. Romero's *Dawn of the Dead* is essential to comprehending the videoludic satire of *Dead Rising* games. To this end, the section demonstrates how Romero's filmic satire is alluded to in Capcom's games. The third section argues that, while *Dead Rising* games allude to the satire of *Dawn of the Dead*, they also recontextualise this satire with their unique story elements. These story elements add nuance to the satire on excessive consumption expressed in *Dead Rising* games by portraying this consumption as symptomatic of post 9/11 marketing strategies and trends. The fourth section then asserts that *Dead Rising* games adapt the ironic dimension of zombie hunger;

DOI: 10.4324/9781003467175-3

this hunger, which can be viewed as an allegory for materialistic consumption, is also depicted as a metaphor for gluttony in these games. Accordingly, this section shows how *Dead Rising* games target food consumption as part of their satire on excessive consumption. In each case, it is stressed that references to terrorism and ravenous food consumption in *Dead Rising* games ensure that these games resonate with twenty-first century audiences.

***Dead Rising*'s Satire and Story Overview**

Satire in *Dead Rising* games is highly specialised in that it targets excess, which it posits as a distinctly American problem. To clarify, the notion of excess that is satirised in *Dead Rising* games is that which can be described as "having too much of something" (Abbott, 2014: 2). To use the words of Bauman: "To be 'in excess' means to be too many, or too much [...] 'Too' signals that something is not really necessary, desirable or pleasing. 'Too' means redundancy; uselessness; waste" (2001: 85). Regarding the target of satire in *Dead Rising* games, excess can be thought of as acquiring (or attempting to acquire) too many material goods or eating too much food. Bauman also contrasts the notion of excess with that of normality. Clearly, excess indicates the violation of a "standard, a norm, a just and proper measure" (Bauman, 2001: 85). This raises the question of what the "proper measure" of something is. In *Dead Rising* games, excessive consumption is consumption that infringes on the avatar's wellbeing and/or responsibilities. Thus, the "proper measure" of consumption in these games is that which negates harm to their avatars and allows the player to progress through their story-based missions, thereby discovering the causes of each game's zombie outbreak.

In *Dead Rising 1*, which released for the Xbox 360 on August 8, 2006, players control Frank West, a photojournalist who travels to the town of Willamette, Colorado, after being informed by an unknown source that something newsworthy is happening there. Arriving at the town's mall by helicopter, Frank discovers that a zombie outbreak has occurred and (player permitting) spends the following three days investigating its cause. This cause is revealed to be a Central American terrorist named Carlito Keyes, with the support of his little sister, Isabela. Carlito orchestrated the zombie outbreak in an act of revenge against the United States of America, which sanctioned the destruction of his hometown, Santa Cabeza. Here, the U.S. government was covertly researching wasp-like insects that turned animals into zombies. This project was led by Dr Russell Barnaby, an elderly man who resided in Willamette at the time of Carlito's attack. Dr Barnaby and his researchers had hoped to develop a means of mass-producing cattle to cater to U.S. citizens' excessive consumption of meat products.

Dead Rising 2 released for the PlayStation 3 and Xbox 360 on September 24, 2010. Its players control Chuck Greene, a former motocross champion partaking in a gladiatorial gameshow called Terror Is Reality. This gameshow involves contestants slaughtering hordes of the undead for sizeable cash prizes, which Chuck needs to afford an expensive drug named Zombrex. This drug is vital to Chuck, as it prevents his infected daughter, Katey, from turning into a zombie. After a show in Fortune City, a Nevada-based resort reminiscent of Las Vegas, zombies are intentionally released from their holding pens. A large-scale zombie outbreak then ensues across Fortune City. Chuck is blamed for the outbreak, which is reported as an act of terrorism by news outlets. Consequently, he must spend the next three days finding evidence of his innocence before a military rescue team arrives.

The zombie outbreak in *Dead Rising 2* was caused by Tyrone King, the host of Terror Is Reality. Having instigated the outbreak, Tyrone attempted to rob Fortune City's casino vaults – the inference here is that his actions were motivated by greed. However, the true villain behind the Fortune City outbreak is later shown to be Phenotrans: the manufacturer of Zombrex. As the undead form an integral part in the development of their drug, Phenotrans needed a fresh supply of zombies to harvest. So, the corporation paid Tyrone to cause the Fortune City outbreak – although, they did not plan for his subsequent looting of the city. Further benefitting Phenotrans, zombie outbreaks create new customers for the corporation, as infected survivors rely on Zombrex to survive. Hence, a macabre cycle of supply and demand is propagated by the pharmaceutical organisation. In October 2011, *Dead Rising 2* was re-imagined as *Dead Rising 2: Off the Record*, a game that released on the PlayStation 3 and Xbox 360. This non-canon game largely replicates the story of its predecessor but has the player control Frank instead of Chuck.

Dead Rising 3 released for the Xbox One on November 22, 2013. The game takes place around 2020 (years after *Dead Rising 2*) and occurs several days into a zombie outbreak in the Californian city of Los Perdidos. Players of *Dead Rising 3* control Nick Ramos, a mechanic who is building a plane to escape Los Perdidos with his friends. He has six days to do this before the U.S. military firebombs the city. The game's zombie outbreak was caused by the U.S. Secretary of Defence and a Phenotrans executive named Marian Mallon. The former aimed to harness zombies as bioweapons, while the latter hoped another zombie outbreak would draw out an immune citizen from which to develop a permanent cure for zombiism. Initially, Marian was reluctant to cause the Los Perdidos outbreak, but she was encouraged to do so by Isabela, who came to work for Phenotrans since the events of *Dead Rising 1*. Nick discovers that he is immune to the zombie contagion and is consequently pursued by Marian and Isabela.

Coinciding with its Christmas aesthetic, *Dead Rising 4* was released for PC and Xbox One on December 6, 2016. The game takes place in Willamette during January of 2022, several weeks after zombies ravaged the newly built Willamette Memorial Megaplex on the day of the Black Friday sales. Players of *Dead Rising 4* once again control Frank, who returns to Willamette to determine the cause of the most recent zombie outbreak. The cause of this outbreak is revealed to be an intelligent zombie called Calder. This zombie was created when soldiers working for a covert military organisation known as Obscuris infiltrated a lab owned by Dr Barnaby. While still human, Calder entered a strange machine inside this lab. The machine, which was developed by Dr Barnaby to create zombies with their brainpower intact, then activated. As a result, Calder was transformed into a unique zombie with retained cognitive abilities. Yet, the process of this transformation drove him insane, leading him to deem the eradication of humanity necessary. With his zombified comrades in tow, Calder left Dr Barnaby's lab and lead an assault on the Willamette Memorial Megaplex.

An Obscuris Commander named Maria Eleanor Raquel Fontana explains why her organisation infiltrated Dr Barnaby's lab. Initially, the group sought to perfect Dr Barnaby's research and sell immortality treatments to wealthy clients. But, having learned of the inadequacy of this research, Obscuris changed their plan. Instead of pursuing immortality, the group made it their mission to exploit the undead. In Fontana's words, Obscuris sought to "pacify, domesticate, and train" (relatively) smart zombies and produce a commercially viable undead workforce. Hence, like Tyrone King and Phenotrans, Obscuris were driven by financial gain.

Dead Rising's Association with George A. Romero's *Dawn of the Dead*

In their satirisation of excessive consumption, *Dead Rising* games strongly evoke *Dawn of the Dead*. The connection between Capcom's games and Romero's film is highlighted by paratextual materials associated with the former, which allude to the latter. Paratextual material describes content that exists outside or on the threshold of a text and contributes to understandings of said text. The concept was introduced by Genette (1997a) to describe the framing aspects of literary publications sanctioned by authors and/or their associates: for example, book titles, prefaces, blurbs, and illustrations. The term is more liberally applied in relation to video games, as researchers often dismiss Genette's criteria of authorial integrity (Švelch, 2020). To clarify, Genette stated that "something is not a paratext unless the author or one of his associates accepts responsibility for it" (1997b: 9). Yet, in video game studies, Genette's criterion is broadened, as paratexts come to encompass anything that is external to gameplay but nonetheless adds meaning to it. Of relevance to satire in *Dead Rising* games are the following paratextual materials: interviews with people who worked on these games, publications pertaining to these games, and menu screens found within these games.

Keiji Inafune, who created the *Dead Rising* series, claimed that he wanted to make a game that "paid homage to the zombie movies of yesteryear, like [those of] Romero" (cited in Villoria, 2006). Additionally, Annie Reid, the writer for several *Dead Rising* games,[1] asserted that *Dead Rising 1* is fundamentally about the United States; as part of her commentary on the DVD featurette, *Terror Is Reality: The Making of Dead Rising 2* (Capcom, 2010),[2] Reid stated that *Dead Rising 1* satirised "American culture" and confirmed the intent of future games in the series to do the same. Moreover, the continued focus on satire in *Dead Rising* games is evident in interviews with staff who worked on *Dead Rising 4*. When asked whether this game would incorporate the drama and "full on satire" (*Electric Playground Network – EPN*, 2016) of its predecessors, executive producer Bryce Cochrane responded in the affirmative. Cochrane even described the interrogation of consumerism as a core theme in the fourth game during an interview for *GamerHubTV* (2016), as did Capcom Vancouver's studio director, Joe Nickolls, in an interview for *GamesIndustry.biz* (Dring, 2016).

Comments made by Inafune, Reid, Cochrane, and Nickolls substantiate the connection between *Dead Rising* games, Romero's oeuvre, and satire. Likewise, they highlight the thematic focus on consumption in *Dead Rising* games. Curiously though, neither Inafune, Reid, Cochrane, nor Nickolls mention *Dawn of the Dead* as a point of reference for *Dead Rising* games. On the contrary, efforts were made by Capcom to distance their series from Romero's film. This is most obvious in the box art for *Dead Rising 1*, which contains a disclaimer stating that the game was "not developed, approved or licensed by the owners or creators of George A. Romero's Dawn of the Dead."[3] In an interview for *Hardcore Gamer Magazine*, Inafune also downplayed the satirical implications of situating *Dead Rising 1* in a mall, suggesting that the locale was selected purely because of its American iconicity: "[g]o to places like London and you've got Big Ben, Paris – the Eiffel Tower, but when it comes to America you've got malls everywhere" (2006: 46).

It could be argued that comments by Capcom and Inafune undermine the connection between *Dead Rising* games and *Dawn of the Dead*. However, this is not the case. Instead, Capcom and Inafune's attempts at distancing their game from Romero's film was likely the result of a legal dispute between Capcom and the MKR Group, who own the rights to *Dawn of the Dead*. While developing *Dead Rising 1*, Capcom were accused of copyright and trademark infringement by the MKR Group on the grounds of their game's similarities to Romero's film. Tensions between the two companies later escalated as Capcom sought an injunction against the MKR Group, declaring the concept of fighting zombies in a shopping mall "wholly unprotectable" (Boyes, 2008). Following this, the MKR Group sued Capcom, triggering the *Capcom Co. v. The MKR Grp., Inc.* lawsuit. In the end, Capcom emerged victoriously from the lawsuit, with United States Magistrate Judge Richard Seeborg dismissing the MKR Group's claims of copyright infringement.[4]

The connection between *Dead Rising* games and *Dawn of the Dead* is highlighted in video game journalism (Navarro, 2006; Rouse, 2016; Reeves, 2019; McWhertor, 2024) and academia (McCrea, 2009: 228; Weise, 2009: 257; Schott, 2011; Jørgensen, 2020: 130). Yet, this connection is most often

Figure 2.1 The menu screen in *Dead Rising 1*.

made on the grounds of the retail-oriented environments in *Dead Rising* games rather than their respective satires. However, menu screens in *Dead Rising* games foreshadow the satire expressed in the games proper. For example, the mall in the first game's menu screen immediately recalls the mall from *Dawn of the Dead* (Figure 2.1). Numerous "SALE" signs pave the way to the building, which zombies shamble towards despite a discernible absence of human survivors to draw them there. Hence, the menu screen for *Dead Rising 1* evokes comments made by Stephen and Peter in *Dawn of the Dead*. Namely, those comments hypothesising that the undead are instinctively drawn to consumer spaces. As such, the Willamette Parkview Mall cannot be read as merely indicative of American iconography, as Inafune suggested. Likewise, the menu screen for *Dead Rising 2* invokes Romero's satire by depicting zombies heading towards an entertainment hub (the Fortune City Arena) without the incentive of human meat consumption.

The menu screen in *Dead Rising 3* shows the ruined city of Los Perdidos in the distance and does not contain any zombies. However, *Dawn of the Dead* is still alluded to by a vandalised road sign that reads "Welcome to HELL." This is reminiscent of another sequence of dialogue from Romero's film. Specifically, Peter's famous line "when there's no more room in hell, the dead will walk the earth." Thus, an intertextual reference to Romero's satirical film is maintained in *Dead Rising 3*'s menu screen. In addition, the menu screen in *Dead Rising 4* flits between multiple scenes depicting the interiors/exteriors of shops. As in the menu screen for *Dead Rising 3*, though, these images lack zombies. However, the presence of these creatures is indicated by visuals that are typical of zombie cinema: crashed cars, burning décor, and blood splatters. Therefore, when conflated with the "SALE" signs reminiscent of those seen in *Dead Rising 1*'s menu screen, the images in *Dead Rising 4*'s menu screen once more call to mind *Dawn of the Dead*'s "zombie consumer[s]" (Loudermilk, 2003: 91).

How *Dead Rising* Recontextualises the Satire of *Dawn of the Dead*

By virtue of their aesthetic qualities, *Dead Rising* games clearly allude to Romero's filmic satire on the false security of consumerism in *Dawn of the Dead.* Yet, they also rework this satire with their unique story elements. These story elements (which are communicated via each game's fictionalised world and cutscenes) frequently refer to terrorism. This allows *Dead Rising* games to maintain popular cultural salience by evoking what was likely the most notable of Western anxieties during the years that the series was active: terrorist attacks (Bishop, 2010: 9). More significantly, though, the emphasis on terrorism in *Dead Rising* games refines their satire; specifically, it facilitates the satirisation of excessive consumption in a manner that recalls and rebukes the "ideology of salvation through consumerism" (Briefel, 2011: 142). According to this ideology, which rose to prominence in the United States after the September 11 terrorist attacks, American citizens should perceive shopping as a means of resisting terrorist threats. *Dead Rising* games, however, subvert this ideology.

The notion of salvation through consumerism was promoted by President George W. Bush in the immediate aftermath of the 9/11 terrorist attacks, which involved four coordinated assaults on the United States by Al-Qaeda. These assaults comprised the hijacking of four passenger planes. Three of these planes were crashed into the Twin Towers of The World Trade Center and the Pentagon. The fourth plane was intended to hit the United States Capitol Building but instead crashed into a field in Pennsylvania after passengers tried to regain control of it. These events occurred between 8:46 a.m. and 10:28 a.m. Later, at 8:30 p.m. on the same day, President Bush addressed the American people, assuring them that "financial institutions remain strong and that the American economy will be open for business as well" (cited in Bindig and Bosau, 2010: 37). Implicitly, then, "in their moment of need, Americans were told by the president of the United States to go shopping" (Bindig and Bosau, 2010: 37). Adding to this, a month after 9/11, President Bush urged the American people not to allow terrorists to succeed in "frightening our nation to the point where we don't [...] conduct business [or] shop" (cited in Scanlon, 2005: 175). This statement explicitly frames shopping as a patriotic act of resistance against terrorist threats and likewise implies that refraining from shopping is an act of submission to terrorists.

The marketisation of 9/11 was discernible in the sale of World Trade Center paraphernalia on eBay after the September 11 terrorist attacks (Heller, 2005: 9). Furthermore, Wal-Mart's American flag sales skyrocketed on the day of these attacks: 116,000 flags were sold, 110,000 more than on the same day a year earlier (Scanlon, 2005: 177). Though, the ideology of salvation through consumerism was perhaps most spectacularly envisioned by the National September 11 Memorial and Museum. This museum, which opened in 2014, came with an accompanying gift shop. Diane Horning, the mother of one of the victims of 9/11, declared it "the crassest, most insensitive thing to have a commercial enterprise at the place where [her] son died" (cited in Edelman, 2014). She even added that she saw the museum as "a money-making venture to support inflated salaries [built] over [her] son's dead body" (cited in Edelman, 2014). Since the museum features an underground storage room containing thousands of unidentified body parts, Horning's claim that the museum encourages commerce over the bodies of 9/11 victims was not figurative either.

It should be noted that post 9/11 consumerism in America is a complex phenomenon that, aside from being read as rooted in capitalist exploitation, can be engaged in and promoted to memorialise the September 11 attacks and to express solidarity in its aftermath (Heller, 2005). Hence, when a wife and husband in Florida spent $7,000 on new furniture, ordered a new roof, and sought to purchase a new car in October 2001, they reportedly did this because they did not "want the terrorists to think they won" (cited in Scanlon, 2005: 176). Also, with regard to the National September 11 Memorial and Museum, media sensationalism concerning the profiteering of the gift shop contrasted with its actual goal: to sustain the museum. Although the items on sale in the museum – plush search and rescue dogs ($20), memorial charms ($65), "In Darkness We Shine Brightest" hoodies ($39) – could easily be interpreted as "tasteless kitsch" (Aguilar, 2014: n.p.).

While the *Dead Rising* do not explicitly refer to 9/11, they consistently depict and mention fictionalised terrorist attacks as a means of recontextualising Romero's satire on the false security of consumerism for contemporary audiences. Thus, the games imply that post 9/11 consumerism is unambiguously and shamelessly opportunistic in its promotion, with its participants depicted as cultural dupes, by way of creating their own terror-ridden worlds. In *Dead Rising 1*, this recontextualisation is communicated through the figure of Carlito Keyes: the Central American terrorist who instigated the Willamette outbreak with the aid of his sister, Isabela. Hence, an act of terrorism is the catalyst for the events of the entire *Dead Rising* series. This ensures that in-game consumption in *Dead Rising* games can easily be paralleled with post 9/11 consumption in the real world. Likewise, in satirising the former, the games can be seen to undermine the latter.

Sustaining their association between in-game consumption and post 9/11 consumption, multiple references to terrorist attacks are made throughout *Dead Rising* games. In a cutscene from *Dead Rising 2*, Chuck Green is accused of initiating the Fortune City outbreak in an act of terrorism, with supporting character Stacey Forsythe proceeding to discuss Carlito's terrorist attack from the prior game. In addition, the "pay-per-view" gameshow, Terror Is Reality, is indicative of the game's satire on post 9/11 opportunism: especially as it was reportedly conceptualised following Inafune's proposition that if the undead were to exist in the real world they would inevitably be transformed into "big business" (Ohara, qtd. in Stratton, 2010: 208). Truly, this gameshow dramatises the words of Heller in *The Selling of 9/11*: that "[t]o the casual observer it might seem that there is no occasion so solemn in the United States – no tragedy so tragic – that it cannot be used for the purposes of short-term commercial profit" (2005: 3). Adding to this, *Dead Rising 3* once again recounts Carlito's terrorist attack in a cutscene where Isabella speaks about Santa Cabeza. Furthermore, the game depicts terrorist-related iconography throughout its setting – iconography that became prominent in American horror cinema after 9/11 (Wetmore, 2012). For example, in Los Perdidos, tall buildings emit clouds of dust and smoke, a commercial plane crashes in a spectacular fashion, and zombies plummet to the ground having fallen from building windows (alluding to The Falling Man).

The topicality of *Dead Rising 3*'s satire on excessive (post 9/11) consumerism is more directly expressed in a location named the Museum of the Americas, where Nick Ramos must venture to progress the game's story. Here, an exhibit dedicated to America's often terrorist-related zombie epidemics is accessible. In this exhibit, a cardboard cut-out of Carlito is present alongside a voice recording describing him as "the Central American terrorist who started the Willamette Outbreak." The fact that this exhibit is situated next to the museum's gift shop calls to mind the infusion of memorialisation and profiteering that was both facilitated and denounced in the aftermath of the September 11 terrorist attacks (Heller, 2005). Interestingly, though, *Dead Rising 3* was released before the opening of the National September 11 Memorial and Museum and its accompanying gift shop. *Dead Rising 4*, however, was released two years after this museum opened and undoubtedly dramatises popular perceptions of it as "callous consumer opportunism" (Aguilar, 2014: n.p.).

In *Dead Rising 4*, the satirical connection between consumption and the exploitation of terrorist atrocities is explicit. While previous titles satirised excessive (post 9/11) consumption by conflating zombies, consumer spaces, and terrorist-related iconography, this game tangibly fuses these elements together with its central location: the Willamette Memorial Megaplex. Essentially, the building is a commercially driven tombstone for those who lost their lives during the events of the first game. Thereby, it is indicative of a culture that deems honouring the memory of those who lost their lives due to terrorism secondary to sustaining vast levels of consumption/profit. The Willamette Memorial Megaplex undeniably embodies notions of post 9/11 profiteering, particularly with regards to Ground Zero's "conspicuous commodity culture" (Potts, 2012: 233) in which tour guides charged "$15 a head to point out the spot where firefighters raised the flag" (Blair, cited in Stone, 2006: 156) and visitors could purchase "twin-tower T-shirts [and] toilet paper bearing the face of Osama Bin Laden" (Stone, 2006). Yet, while the macabre souvenir economy at Ground Zero can be thought of as "a paradigmatic example of the extreme commodification of death and tragedy" (Potts, 2012: 233), the Willamette Memorial Megaplex takes this to new heights.

By depicting the appropriation of a national tragedy as a vehicle for selling commodities on Black Friday, *Dead Rising 4* dramatises post 9/11 commercial opportunism in a way that is even more outlandish than the Terror Is Reality gameshow of *Dead Rising 2*. The seasonal situatedness of the game even alludes to Horning's internationally publicised disdain over the selling of baubles at the National September 11 Memorial and Museum gift shop, which she described as "shocking and repugnant" (cited in Edelman, 2014; Calgary Herald Staff, 2014; Zurcher, 2014). Truly, the Willamette Memorial Megaplex evokes notions of post 9/11 profiteering in the most hyperbolic terms. In this way, the game sustains the series-wide satire on excessive consumption in a way that invokes and criticises the post 9/11 ideology of salvation through consumerism.

How *Dead Rising* Alters the Satire of *Dawn of the Dead*

Dead Rising games were developed and released during a time in which the number of fast-food products made available in the United States was on the rise. Evidencing this, McCrory et al. (2019) gathered data from ten popular fast-food franchises popular in the U.S. to gain an insight into changes to their portion sizes and energy content from 1986 to 2016. This data showed a collective increase of 226% among the foodstuffs available (entrées, sides, and desserts) from all ten restaurants over the 30-year period. This means that customers were frequently given more options relating to what to eat at fast-food outlets between 1986 and 2016. Markedly, there was also an increase in energy (kilocalories) per item in all food groups during this period. Thus, as the choice of what to eat in U.S.-based restaurants increased so did their kilocalorie content. Parallelling these developments were concerns over mass food consumption and the negative impacts it could have on human health and the environment. *Dead Rising* games, then, were developed and released during a time when food-related anxieties were prevalent in the media landscape. Fittingly, as well as satirising the excessive consumption of material goods after 9/11, the *Dead Rising* games also target gluttonous food consumption. They do this by adapting the allegorical nature of zombie hunger from a metaphor for acquisitiveness to a metaphor for excessive eating habits.

From a popular cultural perspective, *Dead Rising* games resonate with a trend among post-millennial zombie fictions whereby these fictions became increasingly preoccupied with the production and excessive consumption of food. Specifically, fast food, which is defined here using the Oxford definition as "easily prepared processed food served in snack bars and restaurants as a quick meal or to be taken away" (cited in McCrory et al., 2019: 1). Positioned against the backdrop of food crisis texts (media that centralised anxieties concerning the sustainability of mass food production/consumption),[5] Newbury (2012) argues that post-millennial zombie films revel in notions of food consumption run amok. Indeed, visualisations of both real and fictional food products and brands abound in zombie films. There is Pepsi, 7-Up, and Tango in *28 Days Later* (Boyle, 2002); Classic Coke and Diet Coke in *Shaun of the Dead* (Wright, 2004); and the fictional Hallowed Grounds coffee brand in *Dawn of the Dead* (Snyder, 2004).

Tying zombie hunger to food production explicitly, Newbury notes how both *Zombieland* (Fleischer, 2009) and *The Simpsons Treehouse of Horror XX* (FOX, 2009) feature zombie outbreaks beginning with the consumption of contaminated burgers. Adding to this, it should be noted that CW's *iZombie* (2015–2019) traces its undead outbreak to the sports drink Max Rager, Netflix's *Santa Clarita Diet* (2017–2019) sees its central character Sheila Hammond (Drew Barrymore) transform into a zombie after eating a dubious clam dish from a local restaurant, and Capcom's *Resident Evil 7: Biohazard* (2017) sees the antagonistic Baker Family force feed their victims chunks of flesh that are implied to contain a mind-controlling (and thereby zombifying) mould. Furthermore, in *Dead Rising* games, food production and consumption are integral to the origin of the undead, as these creatures are by-products of covert experiments pertaining to the cultivation of livestock.

A corelation between zombiism and gluttonous food consumption is established from the beginning of the *Dead Rising* series when Dr Barnaby reveals the motivations of his team of researchers at the U.S.-owned Livestock Research Facility in Santa Cabeza before he dies

> We were…… conducting… experiments to… reduce the costs of breeding… We… accidentally… made zombie livestock… […] We were trying to mass produce cattle. Do you… have any… idea… how much meat… Americans consume… in a single day!? That research… was absolutely necessary!
>
> (*Dead Rising* 1)

The question of how much meat Americans consume daily is left unanswered. Yet, the amount is indicated to be substantial by virtue of Dr Barnaby's impassioned assertion that his research was "absolutely necessary!" Indeed, over 200,000 fast-food locations had been established across the United States before *Dead Rising 1* released. What is more, during this time around a third of consumers considered restaurant and takeaway meals "essential to the way they live" (Paeratakul et al., 2003: 1332). Story information in *Dead Rising 1* thereby satirises this infatuation with food consumption via its backstory on zombiism. In short, the aim of Barnaby's team of scientists was to sustain the vast levels of meat consumption facilitated by U.S. citizens – an aim they ironically achieved by unwittingly creating flesh-eating zombies.

Satire on excessive food consumption is further enforced in *Dead Rising 1* when Frank meets a crazed butcher named Larry Chiang. In his post outbreak delirium, Larry views human survivors as "good meat" to sell on the market. Consequently, he drags the terrorist Carlito to a meat processing room, impales him on a meat hook, and attempts to grind him into human mince. Here, the eating habits of zombies and humans become explicitly intermixed. This further parallels the eating habits of the undead and living humans, insinuating that both are gluttonous consumers of flesh. After Larry is defeated and Carlito is unhooked, the latter once more stresses the game's satire with the following dialogue: "all [zombies] do is eat, and eat, and eat, growing in number … Just like you good red, white and blue Americans." As he speaks, the game's virtual camera pans over an abundance of cattle carcases dangling from hooks. The blood-stained floor makes the room look like the scene of a massacre, such as those caused by the undead. This reinforces the satirical notion that zombie cannibalism alludes to the excessive food consumption of Americans – not just their urge to shop.

Carlito's vendetta against the U.S.A. is regularly mentioned or alluded to in *Dead Rising 1*'s sequels. This not only contributes to their continued recontextualisation of Romero's satire for post 9/11 audiences; it also sustains their adaptation of the symbolic nature of zombie hunger. So, when the Willamette outbreak and the Keyes siblings are mentioned in *Dead Rising 2* by a Terror Is Reality contestant and Stacey, respectively, this serves a double function. It calls to mind the game's satire on excessive consumption with regards to both material goods *and* food – the latter of which is further enforced by a news banner on an in-game news report that announces: "beef consumption is reportedly up for the sixth straight year." Satire on gluttonous food consumption is also evoked directly in *Dead Rising 3* when the context of Carlito's attack is reiterated. This happens when Isabela tells Nick that the American government ordered a lab to be built in her village to "make fatter cattle for [their] fat country to eat." Hence, *Dead Rising 3* upholds the notion of zombie hunger as a metaphor for human gluttony due to Isabela's stereotyping of fat people as overeaters.

Ensuring the satire on excessive food consumption is present throughout the entire series, *Dead Rising 4* re-uses a segment from Carlito's dying monologue as its first line of dialogue. Accordingly, the first words the player hears when starting the game are: "[a]ren't zombies great? I mean, all they do is eat, and eat, and eat." These words echo as Frank has a nightmare about being trapped in the Willamette Parkview Mall. Therefore, despite *Dead Rising 4*'s revision of prior story events (Dr Barnaby's accidental creation of zombiism in Santa Cabeza is transformed into a purposeful one motivated by his research into eternal life, which was conducted under the guise of work on cattle production), the satirical correlation between zombies and U.S. citizens in terms of overeating is maintained and foregrounded.

From Video Game Contexts to Videoludic Satire

Examining contextual information pertaining to a video game strengthens the integrity of claims made about its videoludic satire. Indeed, without addressing this information, it may be difficult to pinpoint exactly what a game satirises. As Fernández-Vara states, "it is always preferable to ground our interpretation [of a game] within building blocks belonging to [its] context area to avoid unfounded interpretations" (2019: 241–2). With regards to videoludic satire, this means it is beneficial to acknowledge the values and ideologies that surround and are embedded within a video game to help determine what the game satirises. Certainly, acknowledging such values and ideologies ensures that any examination of videoludic satire can more accurately pinpoint the rhetorics at play within a game, thereby clarifying which ideas they negotiate, challenge, or perpetuate.

An examination of the contexts pertaining to *Dead Rising* games confirms that they satirise excessive consumption. Furthermore, this examination reveals that *Dead Rising* games accomplish their satire by way of recontextualising and adapting the consumer-critique of Romero's *Dawn of the Dead*. In other words, it confirms that *Dead Rising* games satirise excessive consumption in the form of acquisitiveness and gluttony. Moreover, examining the contexts of these games shows that their satires are imbued with a twenty-first century contemporariness due to their evocations of post 9/11 consumerism and recent trends in zombie fictions concerning food production and consumption. Thus, when *Dead Rising* games target excessive consumption, they simultaneously undermine the American ideology of salvation through consumerism and condemn what they view as America's unsustainable eating habits.

Notes

1 Reid worked as a writer on *Dead Rising 2*, *Dead Rising 2: OTR*, and *Dead Rising 3*.
2 This DVD accompanied special editions of *Dead Rising 2*.
3 The box art of *Dead Rising 1* is easily read as a double-edged (if not sardonic) comment, though, as it simultaneously denies and invites comparability to Romero's film.
4 For a comprehensive overview of the *Capcom Co. v. The MKR Grp., Inc.* Lawsuit, see Wiseman (2020).
5 Notable examples of food crisis texts include Eric Schlosser's book *Fast Food Nation: The Dark Side of the All-American Meal* (2001) and Robert Kenner's documentary film *Food, Inc.* (2009) (see Newbury, 2012).

References

Abbott, A. (2014) 'The Problem of Excess', *Sociological Theory*, 32(1), pp. 1–26. https://doi.org/10.1177/0735275114523419

Aguilar, M. (2014) 'The Tasteless Crap That Fills the 9/11 Museum Gift Shop', *Gizmodo*, 19 May. Available at: https://gizmodo.com/the-tasteless-crap-that-fills-the-9-11-museum-gift-shop-1578479305 (Accessed: 02 December 2023).

Bauman, Z. (2001) 'Excess: An Obituary', *Parallax*, 7(1), pp. 85–91. https://doi.org/10.1080/13534640010015962

Bindig, L. and Bosau, M. (2010) 'Everyday Life: Patriotic Products', in Quay, S. E. and Damico, A. M. (eds.) *September 11 in Popular Culture*. Westport, CT: Greenwood Publishing, pp. 36–8.

Bishop, K. W. (2010) *American Zombie Gothic: The Rise and Fall (and Rise) of the Walking Dead in Popular Culture*. Jefferson, NC: McFarland.

Boyes, E. (2008) 'Dead Rising Brings Lawsuit to Life', *GameSpot*, 28 February. Available at: https://www.gamespot.com/articles/dead-rising-brings-lawsuit-to-life/1100-6186724/ (Accessed: 02 December 2023).

Briefel, A. (2011) '"Shop 'Til You Drop!": Consumerism and Horror', in Briefel, A. and Miller, S. J. (eds.) *Horror After 9/11: World of Fear, Cinema of Terror*. Austin: University of Texas Press, pp. 142–62.

Calgary Herald Staff (2014) 'Families Attack 'Crass' Sale of Souvenirs at 9/11 Museum', *Calgary Herald*, May 19. Available at: https://calgaryherald.com/news/world/families-attack-crass-sale-of-souvenirs-at-911-museum (Accessed: 02 December 2023).

Dring, C. (2016) '"We Need to Make Changes so that there can be a Dead Rising 5, 6 and 7"', *GamesIndustry.biz*, 29 November. Available at: https://www.gamesindustry.biz/articles/2016-11-29-we-need-to-make-changes-so-that-there-can-be-a-dead-rising-5-6-and-7 (Accessed: 02 December 2023).

Edelman, S. (2014) 'The 9/11 Museum's Absurd Gift Shop', *New York Post*, 18 May. Available at: https://nypost.com/2014/05/18/outrage-over-911-museum-gift-shops-crass-souvenirs/ (Accessed: 02 December 2023).

Electric Playground Network (2016) 'Dead Rising 4 What to Expect – Exclusive Interview – Electric Playground', *YouTube*, 30 November. Available at: https://youtu.be/mrJKr-N2NPE (Accessed: 02 December 2023).

Fernández-Vara, C. (2019) *Introduction to Game Analysis*. 2nd edn. New York: Routledge.

GamerHub TV (2016) 'Dead Rising 4 Gameplay Interview', *YouTube*, 29 July. Available at: https://youtu.be/liXuT5ALD78 (Accessed: 02 December 2023).

Genette, G. (1997a) *Palimpsests: Literature in the Second Degree*. Translated from French by C. Newman and C. Doubinsky. Lincoln and London: University of Nebraska Press.

Genette, G. (1997b) *Paratexts: Thresholds of Interpretation*. Translated from French by J. E. Lewin. Cambridge: Cambridge University Press.

Hardcore Gamer Magazine (2006) 'Hardcore Gamer Magazine Volume 1 Issue 12', *Internet Archive*. Available at: https://archive.org/details/hardcore-gamer-magazine-v1i12/page/n21 (Accessed: 02 December 2023).

Heller, D. (2005) *The Selling of 9/11: How a National Tragedy became a Commodity*. Basingstoke: Palgrave Macmillan.

Jørgensen, K. (2020) 'Dead Rising and the Gameworld Zombie', in Webley S. J. and Zackariasson P. (eds.) *The Playful Undead and Video Games: Critical Analyses of Zombies and Gameplay*. New York: Routledge, pp. 126–37.

Loudermilk, A. (2003) "Eating 'Dawn' in the Dark: Zombie desire and commodified identity in George A. Romero's 'Dawn of the Dead'", *Journal of Consumer Culture*, 3(1), pp. 83–108. https://doi.org/10.1177/1469540503003001228

McCrea, C. (2009) 'Gaming's Hauntology: Dead Media in Dead Rising, Siren and Michigan: Report from Hell', in Perron, B. (ed.) *Horror Video Games: Essays on the Fusion of Fear and Play*. Jefferson, NC: McFarland, pp. 220–37.

McCrory, M A., et al. (2019) 'Fast-Food Offerings in the United States in 1986, 1991, and 2016 Show Large Increases in Food Variety, Portion Size, Dietary Energy, and Selected Micronutrients', *Journal of the Academy of Nutrition and Dietetics*, 119(6), pp. 1–11. https://doi.org/10.1016/j.jand.2018.12.004

McWhertor, M. (2024) 'Capcom Just Surprise-Announced a New Dead Rising Remaster', *Polygon*, 26 June. Available at: https://www.polygon.com/24186644/dead-rising-remaster-capcom-release-date (Accessed: 27 June 2024).

Navarro, A. (2006) 'Dead Rising Review', *GameSpot*, 7 August. Available at: https://www.gamespot.com/reviews/dead-rising-review/1900-6155398/ (Accessed: 02 December 2023).

Newbury, M. (2012) 'Fast Zombie/Slow Zombie: Food Writing, Horror Movies, and Agribusiness Apocalypse', *American Literary History*, 24(1), pp. 87–114. https://doi.org/10.1093/alh/ajr055

Paeratakul, S., et al., (2003) 'Fast-Food Consumption among US Adults and Children: Dietary and Nutrient Intake Profile', *Journal of the American Dietetic Association*, 3(10), pp. 1332–38. https://doi.org/10.1016/S0002-8223(03)01086-1

Potts, T. J. (2012) '"Dark Tourism" and the "Kitschification" of 9/11', *Tourist Studies*, 12(3), pp. 232–249. https://doi.org/10.1177/1468797612461083

Reeves, J. (2019) 'In Dead Rising, Dawn of the Dead Came Back to Life', *Doublejump*, 26 November. Available at: https://www.doublejump.co/dead-rising-dawn-of-the-dead/ (Accessed: 02 December 2023).

Scanlon, J. (2005) '"Your Flag Decal Won't Get You Into Heaven Anymore": U.S. Consumers, Wal-Mart, and the Commodification of Patriotism', in Heller, D. (ed.) *The Selling of 9/11: How a National Tragedy became a Commodity*. Basingstoke: Palgrave Macmillan, pp. 174–99.

Schott, G. (2011) 'Digital Dead: Translating the Visceral and Satirical Elements of George A. Romero's Dawn of the Dead to Videogames', in Moreman, C. M. and Rushton, C. J. (eds.) *Zombies Are Us: Essays on the Humanity of the Walking Dead*. Jefferson, NC: McFarland, pp. 141–50.

Rouse, I. (2016) 'Dead Rising (for PC)', *IGN*, 13 October. Available at: https://uk.pcmag.com/pc-games/85366/dead-rising-for-pc (Accessed: 02 December 2023).

Stone, P. R. (2006) 'A Dark Tourism Spectrum: Towards a Typology of Death and Macabre Related Tourist Sites, Attractions and Exhibitions', *Tourism*, 54(2), pp. 145–60. Available at: https://hrcak.srce.hr/161464 (Accessed: 02 December 2023).

Stratton, S. (2010) *Dead Rising 2 Collector's Edition: Prima Official Game Guide*. Roseville: Random House, Inc.

Švelch, J. (2020) 'Paratextuality in Game Studies: A Theoretical Review and Citation Analysis', *Game Studies*, 20(2). Available at: https://gamestudies.org/2002/articles/jan_svelch (Accessed: 02 December 2023).

Terror Is Reality: The Making of Dead Rising 2 (2010) Directed by Capcom <medium>[DVD]</medium>. Canada: Capcom, Blue Castle Games.

Villoria, G. (2006) 'Keiji Inafune Interview', *GameSpy*, 21 February. Available at: https://xbox360.gamespy.com/xbox-360/dead-rising/690415p1.html (Accessed: 02 December 2023).

Weise, M. (2009) 'The Rules of Horror: Procedural Adaptation in Clock Tower, Resident Evil, and Dead Rising', in Perron, B. (ed.) *Horror Video Games: Essays on the Fusion of Fear and Play*. Jefferson, NC: McFarland, pp. 238–66.

Wetmore, K. J. (2012) *Post–9/11 Horror in American Cinema*. London: Continuum.

Wiseman, T. A. (2020) 'The Law of the Playful [Un]Dead: The Influences of Intellectual Property Law on Zombie Video Games', in Webley S. J. and Zackariasson P. (eds.) *The Playful Undead and Video Games: Critical Analyses of Zombies and Gameplay*. New York: Routledge, pp. 246–58.

Zurcher, A. (2014) '9/11 Museum Gift Shop: Hoodies and Anger', *BBC*, May 21. Available at: https://www.bbc.co.uk/news/blogs-echochambers-27496875 (Accessed: 02 December 2023).

3 Spatial Satire

Video game environments facilitate gameplay in several ways: by housing objects that can be interacted with, by providing directional cues, and by confining their delineated gamespaces within discernible boundaries (walls, cliff-edges, forcefields, etc.). Moreover, these environments convey principles and ideologies. As Murray argues, "constructions of game landscapes are revelatory […] because they model systems of engagement that betray values, priorities and biases" (2018: 145). Thus, video game environments can express videoludic satire in the form of spatial satire, which can emerge through the player's explorations of and interactions with *gameworld interfaces*. As explained by Jørgensen (2020: 128), gameworld interfaces encompass the representational and simulated facets of gamespaces. As such, this chapter conceptualises spatial satire in two forms: *aesthetic-based spatial satire* and *affordance-based spatial satire*. The former is conveyed by the visual design of a gameworld (the representational properties gamespace), whereas the latter emerges via the player's interactions with in-game objects (the simulated properties of gamespace).

Consalvo and Dutton's "object inventory" (2006) method of game analysis is useful when conducting analyses of spatial satire. This involves the documentation, categorisation, examination, and subsequent close reading of in-game objects. Consalvo and Dutton allocate their method of game analysis to "objects that can be found, bought, stolen or created" (2006: n.p.). Though, the objects they mention to exemplify their method are small-scale: refrigerators, televisions, artwork, etc. To examine spatial satire, the scope of in-game objects must be broadened. In this respect, objects could comprise entire buildings. This broadening is particularly important for examinations of aesthetic-based spatial satire, which for this chapter involves addressing the satirical implications of structures like *Dead Rising 1*'s Willamette Parkview Mall. Furthermore, the nature of object analyses alters between assessments of aesthetic-based spatial satire and affordance-based spatial satire. For the former, analyses are based on inferences relating to what objects look like. For the latter, analyses are based on inferences relating to what objects can do.

DOI: 10.4324/9781003467175-4

Aesthetic-based Spatial Satire

Attesting to the importance of video game aesthetics, previous scholarship has demonstrated how the design of gameworlds can convey generic verisimilitude (Kirkland, 2009), backstory (Fernández-Vara, 2019), and moral criticism (Green, 2018). Adding to this, aesthetic-based spatial satire shows how fixed facets of gamespace can be read as satirical by way of their world building potential. Ergo, aesthetic-based spatial satire emerges in a similar manner to *embedded narrative*. This term describes "pre-generated narrative content that exists prior to a player's interactions with a game" (Salen and Zimmerman, 2004: 383). However, while embedded narrative can be thought of in conjuncture with cutscenes, as well as in-game documentation and voice recordings (Nae, 2020), aesthetic-based spatial satire concentrates exclusively on information that is entrenched within a video game's architecture and décor.

Aesthetic-based spatial satire manifests through the visual aspects of gamespaces that are often referred to by scholars describing environmental storytelling in games. That is, the organisation of their features and the details ascribed to their *mise-en-scène* (Jenkins and Squire, 2002; Kirkland, 2009). Consequently, recognising aesthetic-based spatial satire requires a level of perceptiveness from the player, who must deduce information from what Green refers to as "environmental clues and details" (2018: 25). Conceptually, then, aesthetic-based spatial satire can be likened to what Fernández-Vara (2011) calls *indexical storytelling*. With indexical storytelling, "the [video game] designer creates the elements of the story and integrates them in the world [while] the player has to interpret them and piece them together" (Fernández-Vara, 2011: n.p.). Similarly, with aesthetic-based spatial satire the designer imbues video game environments with satirical meaning, which can then be read by players through their exploration and close consideration of these environments.

Settings in *Dead Rising* games contain consumer paradises that exude aesthetic-based spatial satire; each game either takes place within or includes a sizeable retail area. There is the Willamette Parkview Mall in *Dead Rising 1*, the Palisades Mall in *Dead Rising 2* and *2: Off The Record*, the Central City shopping district in *Dead Rising 3*, and the Willamette Memorial Megaplex in *Dead Rising 4*. Like the Monroeville Mall in *Dawn of the Dead*, these areas are revealed to be unsustainable from a survivalist perspective. As such, gamespaces in *Dead Rising* games inherently satirise the false security of consumerism. As in Romero's film, the occupation of consumer spaces by zombies attests to the failure of these locales to provide lasting comfort and safety. Also, on their recontextualisation of Romero's filmic satire, this failure undermines the notion of shopping as a form of resistance against, and protection from, terrorist threats. This is especially true of the zombie-filled Palisades Mall, given that the word "palisades" ironically refers to a protective enclosure or fortification. Likewise, individual shops are also indicative of aesthetic-based spatial satire in *Dead Rising* games.

In *Dead Rising 1*, retail spaces are relatively tidy, but in *Dead Rising 2*, *3* and *4* they grow messier. Shelves become emptier and items are strewn across the floor more frequently. The increasingly ransacked look of shops across these games implies that people flocked to obtain the commodities held inside them during their respective zombie outbreaks. This is not surprising, as stockpiling goods is a typical response in times of crisis. During the Covid-19 pandemic, people in the United States and across the world hoarded items that could be deemed essential, like "hand sanitizer, canned foods and toilet paper" (Taylor, 2020). Equally, in *Dead Rising 2*, Roy's Mart contains partially empty shelves that would otherwise be filled with healthcare products and drinks: items that could help survivors endure the zombie outbreak. On the surface, then, the messy aesthetic of this store could be viewed as an attempt by *Dead Rising 2*'s developers to enhance the generic verisimilitude of their game. Yet, healthcare products and drinks are not the only items that have been taken from Roy's Mart. The shelves of the store's cosmetics isle have been raided, too. Here, the nature of the goods pillaged is indicative of something beyond survivalism. Missing beauty products indicate the overwhelming desire of U.S. citizens to indulge in consumer fantasies – to consume in excess rather than taking only what is necessary. By the same token, shirts and shoes are missing from the men's clothing store Modern Businessman in *Dead Rising 2*, handbags and jewellery are missing from the women's clothing store Z & E in *Dead Rising 3*, and technological devices are missing from the electronics store Robsaka Digital in *Dead Rising 4*.

Dead Rising games suggest that a primary response of American citizens during times of crisis is to obtain material goods. Building on this notion, the games satirise crisis-induced acquisitiveness with their inclusion of environmental features that undermine the salvatory power of consumerism. This is made clear in *Dead Rising 3*, which contains the dismembered body of a woman reaching towards a cluster of gems inside Z & E (Figure 3.1). Numerous backstories can be deduced here. Perhaps the woman was attacked by the undead whilst taking advantage of the chaos the zombie outbreak ensued to indulge in a consumer fantasy? Or maybe she was killed after seeking refuge in the store having misplaced her faith in trinkets? Either way, there is clarity to be found in the fact that the items she strived to possess did not save her from the undead. Tellingly of the game's satire, the positioning of her body indicates that her final actions reverse a sequence in *Dawn of the Dead* wherein Peter *removes* his rings so that they do not hinder his shooting ability. In Romero's film, Peter survives because of his ability to reject the allure of material goods (Loudermilk, 2003: 92). On the contrary, the woman in *Dead Rising 3* seems to have died because she could not. Correspondingly, in *Dead Rising 4* the corpse of a man can be found next to a pile of shopping valuables (stylised as Christmas presents) and a treasure chest.[1] The latter is filled with jewellery, and so too signifies a reversal of Peter's actions in *Dawn of the Dead*.

Figure 3.1 The corpse of a woman reaching for a pile of gems inside a shop in *Dead Rising 3*.

In *Dead Rising 4*, satire that targets and subverts the alleged salvatory power of consumerism is conveyed more explicitly in the Willamette Memorial Megaplex. On a conceptual level, the building communicates this satire by way of simultaneously emblematising and undercutting the idea of responding to terrorist atrocities with consumerism. It is a structure that was built to promote commerce in the aftermath of *Dead Rising 1*'s terrorist-initiated zombie outbreak. Equally, it is a structure that failed to serve as a means of resistance against a zombie-led assault on the people of Willamette in the fourth game. In addition, *Dead Rising 4*'s satire is expressed through smaller structures called Zom-B Safe Panic Rooms, which can be found throughout the Willamette Memorial Megaplex and its surrounding areas. These are modelled after real life safe rooms: "standalone or internal shelters that are constructed to protect occupants from man-made threats and natural hazards" (Bounds, 2021: 68).

Demand for safe rooms rose significantly after the September 11 terrorist attacks (Feeney, 2016). However, this demand was not just grounded in the idea of personal safety. It was also motivated by a "Keeping up with the Joneses" mentality. Thereby, purchasing a safe room became indicative of socioeconomic superiority (Bounds, 2021: 68). Accordingly, in *Dead Rising 4* marketing material for Zom-B Safe Panic Rooms emphasises both protection and superfluous spending. For example, posters inside White Rook Security (the store where Zom-B Safe Panic Rooms are purchased) promote "Survival Subscription Plans" and "deluxe walk-in Panic Rooms." Indicative of *Dead Rising 4*'s satire on the false security of consumerism, though, Zom-B Safe Panic Rooms do not protect their users from harm. Some even trap survivors due to what appears to be a flaw in the design of these rooms, wherein they can only be opened from the outside with card keys (which players can search for to free survivors). Moreover, a few Zom-B Safe Panic Rooms contain zombies, indicating that the undead managed to get inside the panic rooms alongside survivors or that infected survivors turned into zombies while occupying the rooms and proceeded to kill their fellow occupants. As a result, these rooms ironically facilitate panic rather than thwart it despite their marketable image as pinnacles of safety and prestige.

Adding to their satire on the false security of consumerism, environments in *Dead Rising* games express aesthetic-based spatial satire on gluttonous food consumption by sardonically representing the abundance of fast-food eateries available in the United States. Entire areas are dedicated to food consumption in *Dead Rising* games, with *Dead Rising 1, 2, 2: Off The Record* and *4* containing their own food courts.[2] Additionally, in a design choice that accentuates their prominence, eateries appear outside of food courts, too. The culinary nomenclature of eateries in *Dead Rising* games reference food that is dense in calories, fat, and sugar. Burgers are referred to in Meaty's Burgers, pizza is referenced in Mr. Chow's Pizza,[3] and confections are referred to in Cheesecake Mania. Attesting to their satire on gluttony, words like "Meaty's" stress culinary excess with their allusions to thickness and fullness. What is more, the word "Mania" refers to a mental illness characterised by bouts of euphoria and uncontrolled behaviour. This suggests that excessive food consumption a commercialised sickness – one that is promoted by the food industry and indulged in by U.S. citizens who refuse to control their appetites.

Emphasising their sense of Americana, the names of eateries in *Dead Rising* games sometimes recall real-world restaurants and cafes that originated from the United States. Respectively, Cheesecake Mania, Pappa Plucky's Fried Chicken, and Pirate's Catch Seafood Restaurant recall The Cheesecake Factory, KFC (Kentucky Fried Chicken), and Long John Silver's. Although, perhaps the most apparent reference to a real-world corporation lies in Hamburger Fiefdom, which alludes to Burger King with its nomenclature and style-based associations with sovereignty. Burger King has historically adopted medieval imagery in its publicity material – the Burger King mascot is a monarch who has been depicted wearing Tudor-era attire since 1976. Customers at the restaurant can even claim paper crowns and (currently) earn virtual ones via an app that can be exchanged for menu items (Burger King, 2023). Burger King's medieval iconography is taken to the extreme with Hamburger Fiefdom, though. Only the name of this restaurant evokes Burger King in *Dead Rising 1*, but in *Dead Rising 2* and *3* the fictional fast-food chain contains decorative knights and medieval typography. There are also banners in *Dead Rising 2*'s Hamburger Fiefdom advertising the "Henry thee "Ate" platter." These banners allude to Henry VIII, a monarch who is recognisable in part due to his substantial size.[4] Consequently, notions of fatness – which is commonly seen as the result of overeating and choosing to have an unhealthy diet (Puhl and Heuer, 2009: 944) – are merged with the food from Hamburger Fiefdom and, by extension, Burger King. Further infusing the locale with notions of commercialised excess, Hamburger Fiefdom makes its final appearance in the form of a grandiose castle in *Dead Rising 4*.

By targeting the false security of (post 9/11) consumerism and gluttony in the United States, aesthetic-based spatial satire in *Dead Rising* games posit the American commercial landscape as one that instils within its citizens a desire for more: more jewellery, more furniture, more home expansions, more food. This is made clear as businesses such as White Rook Security are depicted as opportunistic and exploitative, whereas eateries are seen to facilitate gluttonous behaviour and signify excess with their names and décor. However, *Dead Rising* games ultimately blame American citizens for succumbing to their culturally situated desires to excessively consume. After all, "under neoliberalism, citizens are expected to be responsible for themselves and to govern themselves" (Pérez-Latorre and Oliva, 2017: 791). Thus, while the corpse in *Dead Rising 3*'s Z & E may allude to the victim of a problematic ideology, it also indicates a citizen's death by lack of self-discipline. What is implied here, then, is that the victim would have survived if she had been a responsible neoliberal subject and sought practical items for her current situation. In other words, she would have survived if she had partaken in *rational* consumption rather than what *Dead Rising* games posit as *excessive* consumption.[5]

Affordance-based Spatial Satire

As well as conveying visual information, video game landscapes are imbued with "potentials for actions" (Jenkins and Squire, 2002: 65). In other words, these landscapes encourage players to assess them "in an ongoing, activated manner for [their] use-value or exploitability for success within the rule-based system of play" (Murray, 2018: 180). Regarding affordance-based spatial satire, the use-value of gameworlds is conceptualised in terms of their *affordances*. Broadly speaking, this term describes what an environment can offer an individual. For video games specifically, it describes what gamespace can offer the player. Therefore, affordance-based spatial satire envisages video game space as "ludo-narrative design space" (Aarseth, 2012: n.p.) wherein information is communicated through the player's interactions with game object and environments. In short, it stems from environmental properties that can be moved, equipped, and otherwise utilised during gameplay.

Affordance-based spatial satire can be understood using Pinchbeck's (2009) affordance-based approach to video game analysis. This approach can be used to examine the functions/effects players can extract from in-game objects.[6] For instance, players of *Dead Rising* games can dismember zombies with bladed weapons. Therefore, an affordance of these weapons is to inflict harm on the undead by removing their limbs or heads. Notably, Pinchbeck's approach to video game analysis recognises that the affordances of in-game objects can make players more knowledgeable about the world of a game. That is to say, the affordances of these objects can be imbued with interpretative potential that transcends their use-value. So, to understand affordance-based spatial satire, the functions and effects players can extract from in-game objects should be studied for their satiric implication.

Throughout the *Dead Rising* games, players can direct their avatars to interact with hundreds of in-game objects that consist predominantly of material goods and food. All these objects situate *Dead Rising* games within a broader conception of video games as "simulated shopping experiences" (Pérez-Latorre and Oliva, 2017: 792). In this context, consumerism is often framed positively. For example, in *BioShock Infinite* (2K Games, 2013) "the more things the character/player collects, the better their chances of advancing in the game" (Pérez-Latorre and Oliva, 2017: 792). Yet, it is important to remember that not every video game that showcases a plethora of virtual objects depicts consumption in a positive light, as is exemplified by the general ineffectiveness of a large proportion of goods in *Dead Rising* games. To clarify, these goods could have been programmed to adopt the post 9/11 rhetoric of salvatory consumerism by offering a viable means of defence against zombie hordes. However, they were not. Instead, these goods satirically subvert this rhetoric by proving to be largely futile during the terrorist-associated crises arising in *Dead Rising* games.

Because objects in *Dead Rising* games are unhindered by gatekeeping processes like simulated paywalls, Schott (2011) concludes that *Dead Rising 1* (and by extension its sequels) allows for an idealised vision of consumerism. Specifically, Schott argues that "while the notion of mall-as-utopia is a flawed one for the characters in [Romero's] *Dawn of the Dead*, it works effectively for the player of *Dead Rising* engaging in consumption as play" (2011: 147). However, it is important to remember that consumption in *Dead Rising* games is hampered by the threat of zombies as well as the avatars' limited inventory space, which problematise the ease and magnitude in which objects can be acquired.[7] Likewise, consumption in *Dead Rising* games is problematised by the ineffectual affordances of some in-game objects. For example, vases and potted plants smash immediately if they are thrown or swung at zombies and paintings can be plunged over a zombie's head only once, which merely incapacitates the creature rather than killing it by trapping it within the picture frame (this may seem useful but hindering a single zombie may not provide much relief for avatars given that there are typically hundreds of zombies onscreen). Additionally, objects like gems simply bounce off the undead or cause them to stumble/slip without harming them.

Overall, the affordances of many objects in *Dead Rising* games are less than ideal given the avatar's predicaments. In fact, the affordances of gems corroborate the instance of aesthetic-based spatial satire concerning the woman's corpse in *Dead Rising 3*, which can be seen reaching for these items. The woman's corpse can be read as a warning to players who might themselves be drawn to fetishised commodities. Here, satire derived from the visual representation of a person who died due to their failure to overcome their desire for jewellery could inform the player's gameplay, leading them to avoid suffering the same fate. Or, alternatively, this satire could make them aware of the parallels between the deceased's compromising consumer activities and their own in-game behaviour after discovering the less-than-favourable affordances these objects offer. Either way, *Dead Rising* games do not offer an idealistic vision of consumption as Schott (2011) implies. Indeed, the problematisation of consumption in *Dead Rising* games is crucial to their satire.

Statistical information concerning the damage dealt to enemies by weaponisable objects (typically consumer goods and decorations) in the *Dead Rising* games qualifies their affordance-based spatial satire on the false security of consumption. Thus, as well as being limited by the number of times they can be used, many objects in these games are hampered in their stopping power against threats to the player's avatar. These shortcomings are communicated effectively in the strategy guides for *Dead Rising 2: Off The Record* and *3* (statistical data for the rest of the games is not readily available). In the former, item damage is presented on a scale of one to five, with one signifying the weakest items and five signifying the strongest items. In the latter, item damage is described as low, medium, or high. To make the data from each game more easily comparable, the categories from *Dead Rising 2: Off The Record* can be adapted to match those from *Dead Rising 3*. Hence, the damage rating of zero/one can be considered low damage, whereas two/three can be considered medium damage and four/five considered high damage. Once this translation has taken place, the proportion of each games' categorical percentages are revealed to be very similar, if not identical.

Out of the 255 objects scattered throughout Fortune City in *Dead Rising 2: Off The Record*, 94 (approx. 37%) afford low damage, 136 (approx. 53%) afford medium damage, and 25 (approx. 10%) afford high damage. Out of the 268 objects in *Dead Rising 3*'s Los Perdidos, 111 (approx. 41%) afford low damage, 132 (approx. 49%) afford medium damage, and 25 (approx. 9%) afford high damage. Therefore, around two fifths of the objects available in *Dead Rising 2: Off The Record* and *3* afford little to no damage against enemies. Hence, a large portion of objects in these games do not afford the player's avatar with an adequate means of self-defence. Adding to this, the nature of the objects providing little protection against enemies is significant. For instance, in both games, objects such as gems, toys, and bric-a-brac rank among those providing the least attack power. Alternatively, guns, sledgehammers, and explosives are among objects that afford the most attack power. This indicates an ordering process regarding the objects available in these games, which has its roots in *Dead Rising 1*. As Weise observes, in this game the value of consumer goods shifts towards their usefulness in the context of the game's zombie outbreak: "a lawnmower, a chainsaw, or even a rake is much more valuable than a diamond necklace" (2009: 259). With this value shift, *Dead Rising 1* (and its sequels) proceduralise the survivalist logic that Romero's *Dawn of the Dead* implies. Namely, that in times of crisis items connoting monetary wealth or social status become obsolete.

Clearly, affordance-based spatial satire in *Dead Rising* games undermines superfluous consumption by rendering archaic the player's desire to acquire certain goods (trinkets connoting excess via allusions to monetary wealth and social status). Furthermore, this satire does so while advocating a practical approach to consumption in lieu of dismissing consumption entirely. Consequently, affordance-based spatial satire in *Dead Rising* games adheres to neoliberal values relating to self-discipline and managerial proficiency. As Pérez-Latorre and Oliva state with regards to *BioShock Infinite*, *Dead Rising* games encourage their players to "use [in-game items] strategically and wisely in order to advance in the game" (2017: 791). Players of *Dead Rising* games are thereby urged to control any impulses they may have to seize every item in sight and, instead, only utilise items that are efficient when under threat. Therefore, by attributing different items with different affordances, *Dead Rising* games satirise excessive consumption while simultaneously fostering a pragmatic approach to consumerism.[8]

Dead Rising games do not just encourage the methodical consumption of their in-game material goods by way of affordance-based spatial satire. They also encourage the methodical consumption of in-game food and drink, too. In *Dead Rising 1*, *2*, *2: Off The Record*, and *3* food items can offer negative affordances to the player's avatar.[9] In *Dead Rising 1,* one negative affordance of food consumption is that the player's avatar will receive abdominal cramps. This is conveyed as Frank clutches his stomach in pain. In *Dead Rising 2*, *2: Off The Record*, and *3*, another negative effect is vomiting.[10] These negative affordances can be prompted by the avatar's consumption of "spoiled" foods, such as spoiled meat, spoiled steak, and spoiled bacon. Such items are created after avatars have held onto meat, steak, and bacon for too long. Typically, this takes around 15 minutes in real-time, or three hours of in-game time. Hence, the player is encouraged to be mindful of how long they carry food items, especially those which are prone to expiring rapidly if not stored properly. Sickness is also prompted in *Dead Rising 2*, *2: Off The Record*, and *3* if three or more alcoholic drinks are consumed in quick succession: that is, immediately after one another. These drinks do have restorative effects like other foods when they are consumed in moderation, though.

The negative affordances attributed to eating and drinking in *Dead Rising* games constitute common-sense outcomes to eating spoiled foods and drinking too much alcohol in the real world. Yet, in the context of video games, they violate and satirise the often-unproblematic act of excessive food and drink consumption. For the most part, food and drink in *Dead Rising* games regenerate the avatar's health. This coincides with the typical healing function of such items in video games, which likely stems from the associations between food/drink and nutrition. For example, milk, lemonade, and health drinks can all be consumed by avatars to restore their health in *The Legend of Zelda* series (Nintendo, 1986 to present), the *Pokémon* series (Game Freak, 1996 to present), and the *Silent Hill* series (Konami, 1999 to present), respectively. Likewise, food like cabbages, burgers, and fish can be eaten by the avatar to regain health in *Dead Rising* games. However, in instances where the player directs their avatar to engage in food consumption that the developers behind *Dead Rising* games have deemed problematic, adverse affordances to food consumption are implemented.

Surprisingly, though, negative affordances are not prompted when the avatar is directed to gorge on unspoiled and non-alcoholic food items. So, while contextual story material and non-playable characters satirise gluttonous eating in the United States, affordance-based spatial satire is limited in its proceduralisation of this. On one hand, this appears to indicate *ludonarrative dissonance*: when the narrative and gameplay of a video game express opposing values (Hocking, 2007). From this perspective, the absence of negative affordances when masses of unspoiled and non-alcoholic food items are eaten disrupts the overall satire on gluttony in *Dead Rising* games. On the other hand, the absence of negative affordances when masses of unspoiled and non-alcoholic food items are eaten could be viewed as indicative of the relentless food intake of U.S. citizens; the fact that these items do not prompt illness when consumed could strengthen the games' framing of Americans as unstoppable eaters. Yet, if the latter truly were the case, there would be no need to include negative affordances for any food consumption in the games. Hence, affordance-based spatial satire on excessive food consumption in *Dead Rising* games is discernibly unstable.

Nevertheless, where food consumption does have negative affordances in *Dead Rising* games, health and wellbeing are correlated with lifestyle and consumption choices. This correlation is detectable across a range of neoliberal media. For instance, it can be seen in video games like *BioShock Infinite*, wherein eating fruit enhances the avatar's health and smoking reduces it (Pérez-Latorre and Oliva, 2017: 793). Accordingly, affordance-based spatial satire on gluttony in *Dead Rising* games locates these games within a wider trend that conflates one's personal health with their consumption choices. Of significance to this conflation is its overriding of considerations of health in relation to broader socioeconomic conditions: the widespread availability of junk foods and their perceived cheapness compared to healthier alternatives, for example.[11] Thus, despite corporate food chains encouraging mass consumption with their advertisements and omnipresence across the United States, neoliberal attitudes would place the onus of a population's health on the actions of the individuals within it. Similarly, although aesthetic-based spatial satire in *Dead Rising* games acknowledge that environmental factors encourage gluttony with their parodic fast-food chains and prevalence of food items, affordance-based spatial satire in these games reinforces the idea that a person's health is their own responsibility.

Conclusion

The examination of gameworld interfaces makes it clear that spatial satire can be expressed through the visual design and simulated properties of video game environments. This is apparent in *Dead Rising* games, which express both aesthetic-based and affordance-based spatial satire. Regarding aesthetic-based spatial satire in these games, gameplay environments reproduce *Dawn of the Dead*'s satire on the false security of consumerism by sardonically alluding to, and ultimately undermining, the alleged salvatory potential of post 9/11 consumption. In addition, gameplay environments in these games expand on the satire of Romero's film with their wealth of eateries, which highlight the excesses of twenty-first century food intake in the United States. Regarding affordance-based spatial satire, the multitude of attainable commodities throughout the *Dead Rising* games proceduralise Romero's satire with their minimal and/or limited affordances. Hence, the security of consumerism is falsified by way of the evanescent use-value of these items. Moreover, excessive food consumption is satirised, albeit inconsistently, with negative affordances being attributed to the avatars' consumption of certain food items under certain conditions.

Close consideration of spatial satire in *Dead Rising* games reveals the values these games challenge and promote. Explicitly, these games challenge the desire to indulge in unrestrained consumption by problematising consumer fantasies. Although, this does not mean that they discourage consumption completely. Rather, through their spatial satire, *Dead Rising* games encourage rational consumption: that which is resistant to culturally infused calls to consume excessively. Corpses in *Dead Rising 3* and *4* indicate as much by signifying death by gratuitous consumption, while the plethora of items scattered throughout gamespaces in all *Dead Rising* games reinforce this notion with their affordances. Therefore, on the surface, these games might appear to promote rampant consumption by way of their environmental designs, which centralise consumer spaces and contain a multitude of commodities. Yet, an examination of the satire in *Dead Rising* games reveals the opposite to be true, with a core component of these games amounting to restraint against the drive to consume excessively.

Of course, architecture, décor, and items are not the only aspects of gameworlds. There are also their inhabitants – or non-player characters (NPCs) – to consider. Indeed, Pinchbeck's (2009) affordance-based model for game analysis refers to characters that exhibit artificial intelligence and autonomous behaviours. Pinchbeck calls these characters *independent objects* and *agents*, although for the purpose of consistency this book only adopts the latter term. Such characters, whether stylised as humans, animals, monsters, or robots, can make gameworlds feel like lived-in environments, or transform them into what Jenkins and Squire (2002) refer to as contested spaces. For better or for worse, agents share the world of the game with the player. Besides, they, too, can function as vessels for satire and, thereby, indicate the wider ideological underpinnings of video games. As such, the aptitude of video game agents in expressing satire is explored in the following chapter.

Notes

1 The corpse of the man can be found in the Amazon Food Court inside the Willamette Memorial Megaplex.
2 *Dead Rising 3* does not contain a food court, but it does include restaurants and a butcher's shop.
3 The name Mr Chow also contains a food-related pun, as "chow" is an informal word for food.
4 Henry VIII is known primarily for having six wives, two of whom he ordered to be beheaded, but he is also known for his stature. In fact, Barksdale (2014: n.p.) discloses that the monarch's armour implies that he weighed more than 300 pounds in his later years.
5 While apparent here, the gendered dimension of NPC consumption in *Dead Rising* games is analysed in the proceeding chapter on shared satire.
6 The word "objects" is liberally applied here and refers to a variety of video game components, such as "NPCs […] buildings, barrels [and] health kits" (Pinchbeck, 2009). However, this chapter concentrates on its referral to decorative/useful objects rather than NPCs: the latter are addressed in the next chapter.
7 The number of items an avatar can carry may increase with gameplay progression, although it is always restricted (avatars can never carry infinite items).
8 Even if players do adhere to pragmatic consumption in *Dead Rising* games, affordance-based spatial satire targeting the false security of consumerism is still expressed by way of the fleetingness of objects in these games, as all will break with repeated usage. Therefore, while only a certain number of objects demonstrate affordance-based spatial satire due to their ineffectual combat-proficiency, all objects demonstrate this form of videoludic satire due to their ephemerality.
9 In *Dead Rising 4*, food consumption has no adverse affordances.
10 These affordances can also be viewed as satirical consequences and are thereby discussed further in Chapter 6. To explain, it is the pre-programmed capacity for items to hinder the avatar that imbues them with affordance-based spatial satire, whereas it is the player's decision to trigger these affordances (purposefully or inadvertently) and suffer the consequences of doing so that generates consequential satire.
11 The answer to whether having a healthy diet is more expensive than having an unhealthy diet is complex (Savoie-Roskos et al., 2018). Yet, the fact that *Dead Rising* games sidestep this question entirely remains ideologically significant.

References

Aarseth, E. (2012) 'A Narrative Theory of Games', *Proceedings of the International Conference on the Foundations of Digital Games*, May 2012. https://doi.org/10.1145/2282338.2282365

Barksdale, N. (2014) '8 Things You May Not Know About Henry VIII', *History*, 01 September. Available at: https://www.history.com/news/8-things-you-probably-didnt-know-about-henry-viii (Accessed: 05 December 2023).

Bounds, A. M. (2021) *Bracing for the Apocalypse: An Ethnographic Study of New York's 'Prepper' Subculture*. New York: Routledge.

Burger King (2023) *Royal* Perks. Available at: https://www.bk.com/royalperks (Accessed: 03 December 2023).

Consalvo, M. and Dutton, N. (2006) 'Game Analysis: Developing a Methodological Toolkit for the Qualitative Study of Games', *Game Studies*, 6(1). Available at: https://gamestudies.org/0601/articles/consalvo_dutton (Accessed: 05 December 2023).

Feeney, S. A. (2016) 'Safe Rooms Grow More Popular in High-End NYC Real Estate', *Government Technology*, 19 January. Available at: https://www.govtech.com/em/safety/safe-rooms-grow-more-popular-in-high-end-nyc-real-estate.html (Accessed: 05 December 2023).

Fernández-Vara, C. (2011) 'Game Spaces Speak Volumes: Indexical Storytelling', *Proceedings of DiGRA 2011 Conference: Think Design Play*, Available at: https://www.digra.org/digital-library/publications/game-spaces-speak-volumes-indexical-storytelling/ (Accessed: 05 December 2023).

Fernández-Vara, C. (2019) *Introduction to Game Analysis*. 2nd edn. New York: Routledge.

Green, A. M. (2018) *Storytelling in Video Games: The Art of the Digital Narrative*. Jefferson, NC: McFarland.

Hocking, C. (2007) 'Ludonarrative Dissonance in Bioshock: The Problem of What the Game is About', *Click Nothing*, 07 October. Available at: https://clicknothing.typepad.com/click_nothing/2007/10/ludonarrative-d.html (Accessed: 05 December 2023).

Jenkins, H. and Squire, K. (2002) 'The Art of Contested Spaces', in King, L. (ed.) *Game On: The History and Culture of Video Games*. London: Barbican, pp. 64–75.

Jørgensen, K. (2020) 'Dead Rising and the Gameworld Zombie', in Webley, S. J. and Zackariasson, P. (eds.) The *Playful Undead and Video Games: Critical Analyses of Zombies and Gameplay*. New York, Routledge, pp. 126–37.

Kirkland, E. (2009) 'Storytelling in Survival Horror Video Games', in Perron, B. (ed.) *Horror Video Games: Essays on the Fusion of Fear and Play*. Jefferson, NC: McFarland, pp. 62–78.

Loudermilk, A. (2003) 'Eating "Dawn" in the Dark: Zombie Desire and Commodified Identity in George A. Romero's "Dawn of the Dead"', *Journal of Consumer Culture*, 3(1), pp. 83–108. https://doi.org/10.1177/1469540503003001228

Murray, S. (2018) *On Video Games: The Visual Politics of Race, Gender and Space*. London: I.B. Tauris.

Nae, A. (2020) 'Beyond Cultural Identity: A Critique of Horizon: Zero Dawn as an Entrepreneurial Ecosystem Simulator', *Postmodern Openings*, 11(3), pp. 269–77. https://doi.org/10.18662/po/11.3/213

Pérez-Latorre, Ó. and Oliva, M. (2017) 'Video Games, Dystopia, and Neoliberalism: The Case of BioShock Infinite', *Games and Culture*, 14(7–8). pp. 781–800. https://doi.org/10.1177/1555412017727226

Pinchbeck, D. (2009) 'An Affordance Based Model for Gameplay', *Proceedings of the 2009 DiGRA International* Conference: *Breaking New Ground: Innovation in Games, Play, Practice and Theory*. Available at: https://www.digra.org/digital-library/publications/an-affordance-based-model-for-gameplay/ (Accessed: 05 December 2023).

Puhl, R. M. and Heuer, C. A. (2009) 'The Stigma of Obesity: A Review and Update', *Obesity*, 17(5), pp. 941–64. https://doi.org/10.1038/oby.2008.636

Salen, K. and Zimmerman, E. (2004) *Rules of Play: Game Design Fundamentals*. Cambridge, MA: MIT Press.

Savoie-Roskos, M. R., Jorgensen, M. A. and Durward, C. (2018) 'Does Healthy Eating Cost More?', *Utah State University*, February. Available at: https://extension.usu.edu/nutrition/research/does-healthy-eating-cost-more (Accessed: 17 June 2024).

Schott, G. (2011) 'Digital Dead: Translating the Visceral and Satirical Elements of George A. Romero's Dawn of the Dead to Videogames', in Moreman, C. M. and Rushton, C. J. (eds.) *Zombies Are Us:* Essays *on the Humanity of the Walking Dead.* Jefferson, NC: McFarland, pp. 141–50.

Taylor, C. (2020) 'Here's Why People are Panic Buying and Stockpiling Toilet Paper to Cope with Coronavirus Fears', *CNBC*, 11 March. Available at: https://www.cnbc.com/2020/03/11/heres-why-people-are-panic-buying-and-stockpiling-toilet-paper.html (Accessed: 03 December 2023).

Weise, M. (2009) 'The Rules of Horror: Procedural Adaptation in Clock Tower, Resident Evil, and Dead Rising', in Perron, B. (ed.) *Horror Video Games: Essays on the Fusion of Fear and Play*. Jefferson, NC: McFarland, pp. 238–66.

4 Shared Satire

Calleja (2011) outlines a trio of modes relating to the interplay between video game avatars and agents. These are known as cohabitation, cooperation, and competition/conflict. The first mode conjures a sense of community, the second mode conjures a sense of teamwork, and the third mode conjures a sense of challenge. Given that interactions between avatars and agents can lead to the emergence of videoludic satire in the form of *shared satire*, this chapter introduces three categories that combine shared satire with Calleja's distinctive modes of avatar/agent interaction. These categories are *cohabitational shared satire*, *cooperative shared satire*, and *contesting shared satire* – the latter unifying Calleja's competition/conflict to coincide with his treatment of both as interrelated concepts. Thus, cohabitational shared satire describes satire that emerges from the player's sense of sharing virtual space with agents and even developing a rapport with them; cooperative shared satire arises from instances of collaboration between avatars and agents; and contesting shared satire emerges from instances of competition or conflict between avatars and agents.

To borrow Aarseth's (2012) terminology, when considering the specificities of shared satire, it is irrelevant whether an agent is one of many replicable *bots*, a *shallow character* with minimal characterisation, or a *deep character* with their own backstory. What does matter in this regard is the function of the agent: whether they exist alongside, support, or hinder gameplay activities. As such, shared satire can be detected and documented using a method of game analysis called *interaction mapping* (Consalvo and Dutton, 2006). This involves determining how players can interact with agents as permitted by the rule-based system of a game. Once this is established, the implications of such interactions can be explored.[1] Also, researchers should acknowledge the appearances of agents when examining shared satire. As Weise argues, the rule-based systems of video games are "entirely derived from and reinforced by [their] fictive context [...] which give the rules purpose and coherence" (2009: 240). Therefore, in examinations of shared satire, video game agents should be considered as both *fictional beings* and *game pieces* (Schröter and Thon, 2014). That is to say that their overall character exposition (their

DOI: 10.4324/9781003467175-5

appearances, personality traits, and expressed attitudes during cutscenes and gameplay) should be examined alongside their rule-based patterns of behaviour (how they are programmed to navigate the gameworld, interact with one another, and help or hinder the player's avatar).

This chapter is split into three sections, with each exemplifying and analysing cohabitational shared satire, cooperative shared satire, and contesting shared satire in *Dead Rising* games. In the first two sections, agents known as "survivors" are the primary focus. Typically, survivors are friendly and will facilitate tasks for the player to complete, like fetch-quests and escort missions.[2] With regards to cohabitational and cooperative shared satire, the satirical nature of such missions are examined. In the third section, satire stemming from confrontations with zombies and Psychopaths (human assailants) is explored. On the former, contesting shared satire is expressed through allusions to zombie behaviour in Romero's *Dawn of the Dead*. On the latter, contesting shared satire is conveyed through what the games present as the grotesque eating habits of Americans. In each section, it is argued that agents in *Dead Rising* games provide their fictionalised-American worlds with what Isbister refers to as "local color" (2016: 20). In other words, they give players an insight into the history and values of these worlds. Consequently, the agents examined here reveal much about what is being satirised in *Dead Rising* games, as well as the ideals that these games promote.

Cohabitational Shared Satire

When describing the sense of cohabitation that comes with occupying the same virtual space as agents, Calleja highlights the value of *spectatorship*. In his usage of the term, spectatorship comprises instances where the player's perspective can shift to that of other players, or where the player has an audience in their immediate physical space (when gaming with friends, for example). However, with regards to cohabitational shared satire, spectatorship should be understood as the player observing how video game agents look and behave. It concerns the physiognomy and style of agents, how they interact with their surroundings, and how they interact with each other. These qualities can reveal much about the personalities of agents, as well as the satire they express. Focal points for the emergence of cohabitational shared satire thereby include, for example, agents' clothing, desires, who and/or what they interact with, and how these interactions play out.

Some agents in *Dead Rising* games are portrayed as caricatures of gluttony and acquisitiveness. On caricatures, Sherry (1987) argues that exaggerated depictions of people are not satirical in themselves. Rather, the exaggerated qualities in such depictions of people must allude to a particular stance on their personhood. In other words, they must be rhetorical. Specifically, on representations of fat people,[3] Sherry explains that a caricature of a fat man is not satiric on its own, however, "[a] picture of the same man in front of a table piled high with delicacies is much more likely to be satire" (1987: 12). Satirical caricatures therefore rely on inferences to convey their satire. In the case of Sherry's example, the inference is that the man's weight is due to his dietary choices, which are assumedly fraught with overindulgences. Adding to this, satirical caricatures allude to notions of "ought" and "ought not" (Sherry, 1987: 12). Using Sherry's example once again, the inference is that the man "ought" to reduce his food intake, and that he "ought not" to eat so much.

In *Dead Rising 1*, a videoludic expression of Sherry's hypothetical example of a satirical caricature can be found in the form of Ronald Shiner, an agent who appears after 11 o'clock on Frank's second day inside the Willamette Parkview Mall. Signalling Ronald's appearance, Frank receives a call from a mall employee named Otis Washington, who informs Frank of incidents occurring throughout the building. Otis remarks that he saw a man (Ronald) who looked "pretty overweight" entering a sandwich shop in the Paradise Plaza and even ponders whether he was "just goin' there to get food" rather than seek refuge. After this call, a side mission named Restaurant Man appears on the player's in-game itinerary. Right away, Otis' assumption recalls stereotypes relating to fat people. Namely, that they are excessive eaters (Puhl and Heuer, 2009, Heuer, 2010, and Fruh et al., 2016). Likewise, the title of the side mission emphasises this trait in Ronald by conflating his personhood with a place that is known for preparing and serving food to hungry customers. Therefore, Ronald's depiction as gluttony incarnate is anticipated not only by a proposed correlation between his sizeable body and tendency to overeat, but also by his location.

Verifying the observations and assumptions of Otis, Ronald has a protruding belly that spills over his jeans and dialogue that denotes an obsession with food. Should the player make Frank speak to him, Ronald will demand food and decline Frank's invitation to the safety of the mall's security room unless he is given something to eat. So, to recruit Ronald the player must endanger their avatar by either finding some food in the zombie infested mall and returning it to the agent or relinquishing food in their inventory (should they be in possession of any). Hence, Ronald's hunger differs from that of humans in other zombie-fictions. As Newbury (2012) observes, when survivors engage in candlelight dinners in *28 Days Later* (Boyle, 2002) and Snyder's 2004 remake of *Dawn of the Dead* (as well as in Romero's 1978 original), their mealtimes serve as temporary releases from the horrors of their current situations. What is more, Sublette (2016) claims that these releases are accomplished due to the tendency of such rituals to trigger feelings of nostalgia for pre-outbreak ways of life. In short, human food consumption in zombie films enables survivors to develop communal bonds and fantasise about what once was or what could have been. Likewise, it serves to further distinguish the living from the undead, as the latter eat "without regard to consequence or cultural tradition" (Newbury, 2012: 104). On the contrary, Ronald's hunger does not adhere to such notions of civility. Instead, it satirically indicates that his relationship with food is – much like that of a zombie – one of excess.

A similar side mission to Restaurant Man called Bent Wood features in *Dead Rising 2*. This side mission is triggered if Chuck escorts the professional golfer Luz Palmer to Fortune City's emergency shelter. As a fetch-quest, the gameplay task in Bent Wood is practically identical to the one appearing in Restaurant Man. However, the cohabitational shared satire expressed in Bent Wood targets acquisitiveness rather than gluttony. This is made apparent when Luz's dialogue is triggered. Initially, Luz reveals that she is troubled due to the loss of her "favorite" golf club. Then, she asks Chuck to fetch her a new golf club, adding that she "spotted some real nice ones in the sports shops." Luz's desire to attain material goods mirrors Ronald's desire to attain food in the sense that both supersede each agent's regard for the avatar's safety. Of course, items like golf clubs can be used as weapons in *Dead Rising* games and are therefore useful against the undead. Yet, in stating that she lost her "favorite" golf club, Luz implies that she is in possession of others and does not necessarily require another. Moreover, her reflection on the "real nice ones" she spotted in the shops suggests that her desire for a new golf club is rooted in their aesthetic qualities rather than their practicality.

As well as satirising acquisitive behaviour, Luz's preoccupation with consumer goods reproduces the stereotype of the woman as neurotic shopper. This stereotype can be viewed as part of a wider landscape of "controlling images" – that is, images that justify oppression (Sandlin and Maudlin, 2012: 176).[4] Hence, the stereotype works to justify the oppression of women by depicting them as unrestrained and in need of control (by men). Luz's disregard for the avatar's welfare and yearning for a new golf club during an intensive time of upheaval thereby situates her firmly within an "overtly negative discourse that positions women as irrational, capricious dupes of advertising and of the ideologies of consumerism" (Sandlin and Maudlin, 2012: 180). This stereotype of the woman as neurotic shopper is thought to have arisen in the mid-nineteenth century out of fears that women were "eluding patriarchy's gaze and grip" (Sandlin and Maudlin, 2012: 181) by moving out of the *private sphere* of home life and into the *public sphere* of department stores. A recurring image of the "hysterical female shopper" (Sandlin and Maudlin, 2012: 181) consequently emerged in popular cultural discourse as a reactionary response to the perceived increase in the agency of women. In the context of *Dead Rising 2*, though, such imagery is used as a means of satirising consumer excess and, by extension, furthering the game's advocacy for self-discipline. As such, it works primarily to infer that Luz "ought not" to be preoccupied with material goods and, like Ronald before her, she "ought" to cultivate a sense of control over her desire to consume, even if this desire is culturally instilled within her.

Cooperative Shared Satire

Cooperative shared satire occurs during sequences of gameplay where teamwork is essential: this may be the case in scenarios where the player is required to overcome enemies, obstacles, or complex puzzles. To demonstrate the necessity of cooperation in some video games, Calleja (2011: 105) highlights the dependency of the player on agents in the post-apocalyptic, first-person shooter, *Left 4 Dead* (Valve, 2008). In this game, an AI director generates tension by spawning hordes of zombified enemies to attack avatars and agents at various intervals. Therefore, cooperation in this game is crucial to overcome the undead. It is in the players' best interests to engage in cooperative play by rescuing other player's avatars and game-controlled agents in the hopes that they will return the favour, should they ever need to. In short, cooperative play in *Left 4 Dead* aids in the survival of the player's avatar and their allies. Yet, where cooperative shared satire is concerned, the avatar/agent relationship is not always one of mutual support.

Cooperative shared satire can emerge through gameplay wherein, despite being accompanied by agents, the avatar is left with the brunt of the workload to fulfil in-game tasks; it can arise from agents counterproductively making it more difficult for the player to fulfil gameplay tasks, even if these tasks have been set by the agents themselves. In *Dead Rising 2*, such a situation occurs during the Shopping Spree side mission (Figure 4.1). In this side mission, much like Luz, agents Bessie Kent, Rosa Collins, and Erica Mayes prioritise shopping over the avatar's (and their own) safety. Equally, like Luz, these agents are first encountered in a store that sells clothing and accessories. However, as a point of departure from Bent Wood (or Restaurant Man), the Shopping Spree side mission requires the avatar to escort Bessie, Rosa, and Erica to the safety of Fortune

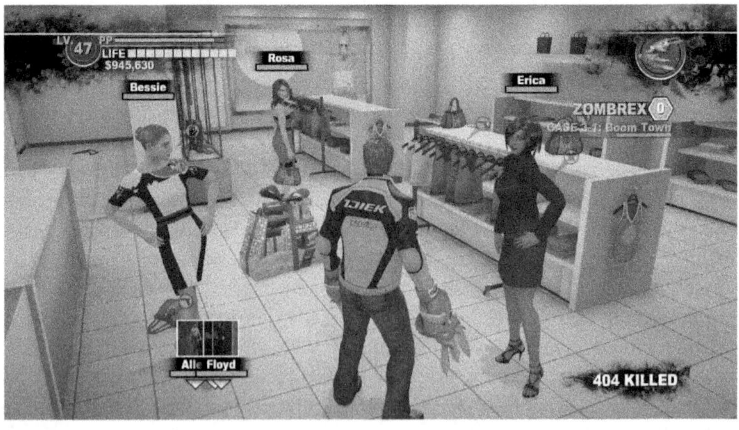

Figure 4.1 The beginning of the Shopping Spree side mission in *Dead Rising 2*.

City's emergency shelter. As is typical of survivors in the *Dead Rising 2*, the women are able form a coalition with Chuck to stay alive. In this instance, though, their cooperative efforts to reach the emergency shelter are hampered significantly by the acquisitiveness of the three women.

Bessie, Rosa, and Erica are recruited simultaneously after the player exhausts the dialogue of one of them. While each woman facilitates a unique exchange, all three foreground the same topic: shopping. "Zombies or no zombies, Kathy's Space was having a sale, and it will take more than the undead to stop me. I just bought the cutest new pumps," asserts Bessie. "When the outbreak happened, we figured there wouldn't be any lineups at the mall, so we went shopping" reveals Rosa. "I got such a good price on those shoes there was NO WAY I was leaving them here," exclaims Erica. Evidently, the trio are emblematic of the consumer delirium that the *Dead Rising* series satirises with their emphases on shopping for clothing items. What is more, the way in which *Dead Rising 2* constructs its satire here is clearly gendered. On consumer stereotypes, Sandlin and Maudlin state that the "narcissistic" and "out-of-control" woman is contrasted with the "rational, autonomous, calculating economic man" (2012: 181). Correspondingly, Bessie, Rosa, and Erica stand in sharp contrast with that of male agents found in Fortune City's shops. For instance, Gordon Dawkins hides inside Casual Gals out of fear of being killed by zombies; Jared Davis builds a barricade around himself with consumer trinkets inside Wily Travels to keep the undead at bay; Jack Ellis and Kenneth Walsh reside inside the hunting store, Shanks, with the former brandishing a bowie knife that he presumably picked up there as a means of self-defence. In these instances, the men's situatedness and claiming of goods does not satirise acquisitiveness because their consumption is framed as rational and pragmatic. On the contrary, that of the women is framed as impulsive, frivolous, and centred around their appearance.

Notably, Bessie, Rosa, and Erica's satirical tunnel-vision for material goods transcends their construction as *fictional beings* and is incorporated into their functionality as *game pieces*. In other words, their acquisitiveness is expressed through their coded behaviours during the gameplay scenario they prompt. Typically, when survivors are recruited by Chuck in *Dead Rising 2*, they aid in his fight against the undead until dropped off at the emergency shelter. This is because they share a common goal with the avatar: to survive the zombie onslaught. Although, this is not entirely the case in the Shopping Spree side mission, as Bessie, Rosa, and Erica only agree to accompany Chuck if he carries their "shopping valuables" – a large collection of packaged goods wrapped in a red bow. As a result, cooperative shared satire manifests through the proceduralisation of the women's self-destructive obsession with shopping, which in turn makes the player's job of ensuring their safety much more tedious than with most other survivors.

Usually, after being recruited survivors will follow the avatar and adhere to directional commands. For example, the player can set waypoints for survivors to follow by holding down the left trigger and pressing the Y button. This causes the avatar to influence survivors by shouting "Head that way!," for example. By contrast, Bessie, Rosa, and Erica violate these rules, as it is only when the avatar takes hold of their shopping valuables that they will accompany him. In this way, the trio pursue their consumer goods rather than the avatar themselves. Likewise, the women refuse to follow directional commands, shouting back at the avatar with exclamations such as "Absolutely not!" in response to his instructions – the prospect of being separated from their possessions clearly distresses them. Once again, this effectively communicates the "ought" and "ought not" implications of shared satire in *Dead Rising 2*. Like Fran and Peter in Romero's *Dawn of the Dead*, the women "ought" to exercise restraint and relinquish their consumer desires. Like Roger and Stephen in the same film, they "ought not" not succumb to the mesmerising pull of consumerism.

For the satire of Shopping Spree to emerge fully, the player must acquiesce to the actions being satirised. They must submit to the demands of Bessie, Rosa, and Erica and direct their avatar to carry the women's shopping to the emergency shelter. This is a burdensome task, as the shopping valuables cannot be stored in an inventory slot due to their substantial size (unlike most other items in the game). Instead, the collective of commodities must be carried by the avatar, who can only hold one item at a time. Large items, such as the shopping valuables, can be used as weapons though. However, should the avatar be made to swing or throw this clump of packaged goods at the undead, Bessie, Rosa, and Erica will vocally disparage him ("You clumsy oaf!") and may also hit him. To make matters worse, if one of the women hits the avatar as he is holding the shopping valuables the goods will escape his grasp. As a result, the shopping valuables can be unintentionally flung into a cluster of zombies, which the women will run towards without hesitation. This means that the player must refrain from attacking the undead with the shopping valuables, even though they may typically do this with other large items. Due to the increase in difficulty that comes as the player strives to guide their avatar and his recruits to the safety of the emergency shelter, the preservation of Bessie, Rosa, and Erica's shopping is clearly depicted as ridiculous.

The incorporation of the player's avatar in *Dead Rising 2*'s cooperative shared satire facilitates the legitimisation of a value pertaining to neoliberalism that was not accentuated during their encounters with Luz or Ronald: individualism. Neoliberalism legitimises the idea that people should be responsible for, and able to look after, themselves (Pérez-Latorre and Oliva, 2017: 790). Thereby, by expressing cooperative shared satire through Bessie, Rosa, and Erica's consumption-driven lack of support for the player's avatar, *Dead Rising 2* frames collectivism as difficult at best. Furthermore, the women endanger themselves via their dependency on the will of others to assist them. Offering an analogy to neoliberalism's demand of individualism, Bailes asserts that "drug addicts, for example, are contemptible not because taking drugs is totally unacceptable (freedom to seek pleasure is one of neoliberal culture's core ideals), but because they cannot fulfil all the demands of self-sufficiency" (2019: 16). In the same way, *Dead Rising 2*'s Bessie, Rosa, and Erica are not contemptible because consumerism is deplorable – as pointed out in the previous chapter, the acquisition of goods is essential to gameplay progression – but because their fixation on consumerism has left them unable to fend for themselves.

Contesting Shared Satire

A potential alteration in the relationship between Chuck and the women of the Shopping Spree side mission has the capacity to alter the form of shared satire these agents enable. This manifests momentarily in instances where Bessie, Rosa, and Erica hit Chuck and emerges fully if the trio's shopping valuables are destroyed. Should this happen, a banner will appear across the screen to notify the player that the agents have "defected." In other words, Bessie, Rosa, and Erica will no longer cooperate with Chuck. Instead, they will become irreversibly volatile and try to kill him. In *Dead Rising* games, survivors typically revolt against avatars if the latter assault them. Thus, in such instances, the violence of survivors can be viewed as self-defence. Alternatively, should Bessie, Rosa, and Erica attack Chuck due to the loss of their shopping, their violence can be read as further evidence of their retail-associated delirium. Hence, their actions will once again reproduce notions of (women) consumers as "emotional and duped" (Sandlin and Maudlin, 2012: 181) to satirise excessive consumption and champion self-discipline and individualism. Accordingly, interactions between *Dead Rising 2*'s avatar and the agents of the Shopping Spree side mission have the capacity to produce contesting shared satire as well as cooperative shared satire.

Contesting shared satire evokes what Caillois (1961) referred to as *agôn*: a form of gameplay wherein players compete for superiority. However, under Caillois' conceptualisation of *agôn* competition is deemed fair due to the artificial creation of an "equality of chances" (1961: 14). Although, with regards to contesting shared satire this equality of chances is not required. What matters here is merely the fact that there is a competition/conflict, no matter how fair or unfair the competition/conflict is. In video games, the scope of competitive activities is broad. For example, players can experience all manner of activities from "[simulated] tabletop games like cards, board games, and strategic war games, to [simulated] physical contests like football, basketball, and other sports, [and simulated] nonsportive contests like gunfights, aerial dogfights, or medieval sword fighting" (Calleja, 2011: 108). Fantastical conflicts may also occur in video games, such as the struggle of avatars against demons and monstrous creatures. Due to the perceivably satirical ways in which avatars and agents can interact with one another, contesting shared satire can emerge through any such competition/conflict in a video game. For instance, in *Dead*

Figure 4.2 Zombies parodying shoppers in *Dead Rising 1*.

Rising games, contesting shared satire is expressed through the abject and deeper allegorical meanings of the avatar's interactions with the undead.

In *Dead Rising* games, contesting shared satire is expressed through zombies because the representation of these creatures as *fictional beings* imbues their functionality as *game pieces* with additional meaning. As such, the conflict that zombies enable should be understood as more than just an opportunity for the player to engage in guilt-free, gratuitous violence, as is often implied of zombies in video games generally (Krzywinska, 2008).[5] Indeed, Kirkland (2016) proposes that encounters with the undead in video games evoke "understandings [...] concerning the nature of the creatures, drawn from zombie films, television, and comic books, as well as other video games" (232). This is certainly true of the zombies in *Dead Rising* games given their evocations of those from *Dawn of the Dead*. In Romero's film, the relentless hunger of zombies makes them "perfect allegorical figures for consumerism" (Bishop, 2010: 139). Likewise, the same can be said of zombies in *Dead Rising* games. Evidencing this, the satirical ties between zombies as consumers is foregrounded early in *Dead Rising 1* during a cutscene wherein the undead clamour against the doors of the Willamette Parkview Mall (Figure 4.2). This cutscene recalls a sequence in *Dawn of the Dead* where zombies can be seen "pressed up against glass doors and windows, clamouring to get inside the shops, in a gross parody of early-morning-sale shoppers, to resume their earthy activities of gluttonous consumption" (Bishop, 2010: 139–40). Consequently, the pre-programmed nature of the undead in *Dead Rising 1* expresses the satirical metaphor of zombies as consumers (and consumers as zombies) in the form of contesting shared satire when zombies try to bite and eat avatars and agents.[6] Truly, this metaphor is maintained throughout this game and its sequels due to their persistent depiction of zombies occupying consumer spaces.

In addition to reproducing and recontextualising Romero's satire on American consumerism, undead enemies in *Dead Rising* games also satirise unrestrained food consumption. As series creator Keiji Inafune has stated, zombies in *Dead Rising* games are symbolic "of mankind's greed, of their desire to eat, of their hunger" (cited in Villoria, 2006). To reiterate, the origin of the undead as creatures created by scientists attempting to mass produce cattle for consumption is regularly mentioned or alluded to in *Dead Rising* games. This means that the attempts of zombies to cannibalise the human avatars and agents in these games must also be read as instances of contesting shared satire targeting the alleged infatuation of American citizens with excessive food consumption. Yet, it should be noted that zombies are not the only in-game enemies to convey this satire. Aggressive agents known as Psychopaths express contesting shared satire that targets gluttony, too. Furthermore, by expressing this satire, Psychopaths also condemn a lack of self-discipline when it comes to dietary choices.

Like the undead, Psychopaths Larry Chiang (a butcher from *Dead Rising 1*) and Antoine Thomas (a chef from *Dead Rising 2*) practice cannibalism, as is foregrounded in cutscenes. Larry drags the terrorist Carlito to the Willamette Mall's meat processing area and attempts to grind him into mincemeat, while Antoine attempts to make "the ultimate dish" from human meat to serve in his restaurant. During gameplay, Larry can pick up the avatar, impale him on a meat hook, and slice at his body with a meat cleaver as though he were carving animal meat. Alternatively, Antoine can climb onto the avatar and force an apple into his mouth, choking him whilst making him resemble a traditionally roasted pig (which is often served with an apple in its mouth). As with Ronald, Larry and Antoine's culinary desires demonstrate a type of food consumption that transcends survivalist necessity, especially as their found locations contain food and drink items already. To reiterate, their attempts at meat consumption do not strive towards post-outbreak sophistication (Newbury, 2012) or involve reminiscing over pre-outbreak times (Sublette, 2016). Instead, their representational and simulated attempts at making a meal of other survivors parallel them even more closely with the undead than was the case with Ronald. Moreover, as condemnatory exemplifications of human gluttony, their large bodies once again show how *Dead Rising* games draw on stereotypes relating to fat people to express their satire on gluttonous food consumption.

Even with their cannibalistic tendencies, neither Larry nor Antoine demonstrate *reductio ad absurdum*[7] quite like *Dead Rising 3*'s Darlene Fleischermacher, a Psychopath whose very name – which translates from German to *butcher* in English – conflates food and death. Psychopaths in *Dead Rising 3* represent the seven deadly sins, with Darlene standing in for gluttony. Fittingly, she is encountered during the game's All You Can Eat side mission, the

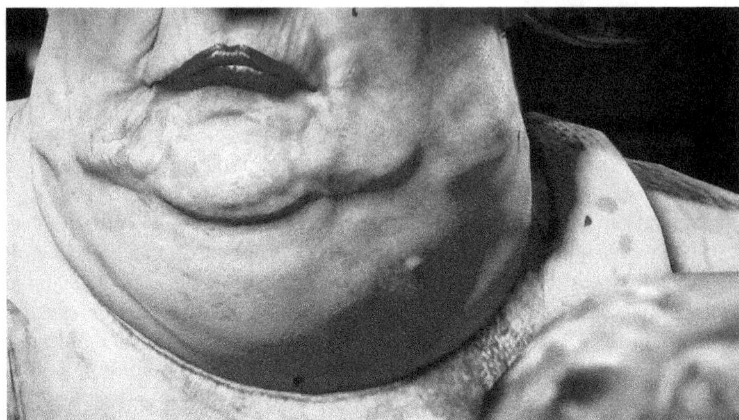

Figure 4.3 An extreme close-up of Darlene Fleischermacher in *Dead Rising 3*.

title of which immediately foreshadows her depiction as a gluttonous *fictional being*. Adding to this, food stains are visible all over her clothes, which consist of a bib stylised with the image of a lobster and a bright yellow dress pattered with a cupcake design. As for her bodily form, Darlene is enormous – so big that she is bound to a motor scooter. In her introductory cutscene, the virtual camera lingers on a shot of her mouth as she bites into a hunk of animal meat (Figure 4.3). She does not desire to eat humans, as Larry and Antoine do, but the extreme close-up of Darlene tearing flesh from bone unmistakably recalls the voracious consumption of the living by the undead. Adding to this, during gameplay Darlene can assault the avatar, Nick, by vomiting on him, thereby mirroring an attack performed by mutated zombies in *Dead Rising 2* (these monsters project harmful viscera from their mouths).[8]

The notion that excessive eating is harmful and that one should exercise restraint against it is communicated by way of the avatar's methods of attack against Darlene. Occasionally, Darlene will retreat to one of the many food serving stations inside her found location, Uncle Billy's Buffet, to vigorously eat after taking damage. This will restore her health points, as it does when the avatar consumes food items. However, eating also leaves Darlene vulnerable to attack. This is made clear via the appearance of a button pressing cue that hovers over her body, highlighting the Xbox One controller's Y and B buttons. Should the player push these buttons, an optional sequence will arise. During this sequence the player is prompted to press X or A repeatedly to make Nick force excessive amounts of food into Darlene's throat, choking her in the process. This prevents Darlene from regaining more health and causes her to vomit profusely – this time causing her damage. Here, the satire on gluttonous food consumption that is conveyed through affordance-based spatial satire (whereby food has harmful affordances when eaten irrationally or excessively) is echoed in *Dead Rising 3*'s contesting shared satire.

Once the player whittles Darlene's health points down to zero, a cutscene reveals her gluttonous behaviour and lack dietary discipline to be the cause of her death. In this cutscene, Darlene skids on her own bile and, unable to lift herself into an upright position, dies of asphyxiation. At the point of her death, she also releases pent-up flatulence as the Nick looks away bashfully. Thus, the battle between the Nick and Darlene ends on a darkly comic and ironic note as the latter chokes to death on the very food she chose to eat in abundance. To clarify, Darlene's death by asphyxiation is not caused by Nick force-feeding her but is inferred to be the result of her choice to overeat; the quick-time event in which Nick can force-feed Darlene is optional and does not need to be triggered to defeat her. Overall, then, contesting shared satire is expressed through the construction of Darlene as both a *fictional being* and *game piece*, with both constructions indicating that she has a lack of self-control when it comes to eating. Additionally, the humour in Darlene's death perpetuates ideas pertinent to *fattertainment* – that is, "media that is both immensely popular and a breeding ground for obesity stereotypes" (Heuer, 2010). Namely, that the stigmatisation of fat people is justified on the grounds that "people are in control of what happens to them and they get what they deserve [...] including laughter and humiliation" (Heuer, 2010).

Conclusion

Video game agents can function as communicative vessels for cohabitational, cooperative, and contesting shared satire. Each of these forms of shared satire relies on the representational and simulated qualities of video game agents. This is made clear as the aesthetic, dialogue, and story information attributed to these agents contextualises their interplay with avatars as satiric in *Dead Rising* games. Thus, by considering agents as *fictional beings*, meaning can be derived from their functions as *game pieces*. Essentially, shared satire can be expressed through an agent's visual aspects and rule-based patterns of behaviour, both of which inform one another. Moreover, examinations of shared satire prove useful in determining what a video game posits as right and wrong via the implication of an "ought" and "ought not," or by the grotesque exaggeration and ridicule of an agent's flaws.

Many agents in *Dead Rising* games satirise excessive consumption. By examining the shared satire these agents exhibit and facilitate, it is made clear that the critiques these games convey are formulated by drawing on clichéd notions of fat people as overeaters and women as out-of-control shoppers. Adding to this, consideration of the "ought" and "ought not" inferences of agents in *Dead Rising* games reveals that these games promote self-discipline and individualism. Thus, in applying the schema of shared satire to discernibly satirical video games, the ideological inferences of these games can be brought to the forefront. With regards to *Dead Rising* games, these inferences point towards an inherently hegemonic standing – one that perpetuates neoliberal values.

Like the previous chapter on spatial satire, this chapter has focused primarily on the visual and simulated properties of video game objects: in this instance, agents. Yet, these are not the only contributing factors when it comes to the communication of videoludic satire. Sound must also be considered. Accordingly, the following chapter examines the satirical use of sound in *Dead Rising* games. In other words, it examines auditory satire. In *Dead Rising* games, auditory satire and shared satire exist in tandem with spatial satire. This is unsurprising, as all modes of videoludic satire in these games target excessive consumption. However, while this chapter has clarified that shared satire expands on spatial satire (via agents modelling the behavioural patterns hinted at in the game's environmental designs), the next chapter demonstrates how auditory satire strengthens, and provides an additional context for, the emergence of spatial satire.

Notes

1 For example, using interaction mapping, Consalvo and Dutton (2006) observe that characters in *The Sims* (Electronic Arts, 2000) must be friends before they can have romantic and sexual relationships. As a result, they determine that *The Sims* depicts a conservative view of courtship that rejects hook-up culture.

2 Fetch-quests involve an agent requesting an item, which the player must find and give to them. Escort missions involve leading agents to designated locations whilst ensuring that they are protected from harm.

3 In alignment with discourse on fat studies – "a field of scholarship that critically examines societal attitudes about body weight and appearance, and that advocates equality for all people with respect to body size" (Rothblum, 2012: 3) – the word "fat" is used in this book instead of other words like "obese" or "overweight." This is because the latter words imply an ideal weight that privileges slim bodies (Rothblum, 2012: 3).

4 The concept of controlling images was introduced by Patricia Hill Collins (cited in Sandlin and Maudlin, 2012: 183–4), who explored how popular cultural depictions of Black women have contributed to the oppression of this marginalised group.

5 This is not to say that the pleasure of zombie killing is not an important feature in zombie-based video games. Indeed, it is one of the core aspects of gameplay in *Dead Rising* games and is even discernibly satirical, as argued in this book's chapter on temporal satire.

6 Satire on U.S. citizens' drive to shop is also apparent during instances where zombies can be found pushing shopping trolleys throughout the Willamette Parkview Mall. As mentioned in the introduction of this book, these zombies serve as more literalised depiction of zombified shoppers. The satire expressed here is classed as cohabitational shared satire, though, as trolley pushing zombies pose no threat to the avatar and merely occupy the same space as them.

7 This term describes an "extreme form of exaggeration" that "may magnify one fault of a character to the exclusion of all other qualities" (Feinberg, 1967: 112).

8 The act of vomiting indicates eating more than one can handle even without its allusions to the ever-consuming undead.

References

Aarseth, E. (2012) 'A Narrative Theory of Games', *Proceedings of the International Conference on the Foundations of Digital Games*, May 2012. https://doi.org/10.1145/2282338.2282365

Bailes, J. (2019) *Ideology and the Virtual City: Videogames, Power Fantasies, and Neoliberalism*. Winchester: Zero Books.

Bishop, K. W. (2010) *American Zombie Gothic: The Rise and Fall (and Rise) of the Walking Dead in Popular Culture*. Jefferson, NC: McFarland.

Caillois, R. (1961) *Man, Play and Games*. Translated by Meyer Barash. Urbana: University of Illinois Press. Reprinted in 2001.

Calleja, G. (2011) *In-Game: From Immersion to Incorporation*. Cambridge, MA: MIT Press.

Consalvo, M. and Dutton, N. (2006) 'Game Analysis: Developing a Methodological Toolkit for the Qualitative Study of Games', *Game Studies*, 6(1). Available at: https://gamestudies.org/0601/articles/consalvo_dutton (Accessed: 5 December 2023).

Feinberg, L. (1967) Introduction *to Satire*. Reprint, Santa Fe, NM: Pilgrims Process, Inc. Reprinted in 2008.

Fruh, S. M., Nadglowski, J., Hall, H. R., Davis, S. L., Crook, E. D. and Zlomke, K. (2016) 'Obesity Stigma and Bias', *The Journal for Nurse Practitioners*, 12(7), pp. 425–32. https://doi.org/10.1016/j.nurpra.2016.05.013

Heuer, C. A. (2010) '"Fattertainment" – Obesity in the Media. The Obesity Action Coalition (OAC)' [online]. Available at: https://www.obesityaction.org/community/article-library/fattertainment-obesity-inthe-media/ (Accessed: 18 May 2019).

Isbister, K. (2016) *How Games Move Us: Emotion by Design*. Cambridge, MA: MIT Press.

Kirkland, E. (2016) 'Undead Avatars: The Zombie in Horror Video Games', in Fischer-Hornung, D. and Mueller, M. (eds.) *Vampires and Zombies: Transcultural Migrations and Transnational Interpretations*. Jackson: University Press of Mississippi, pp. 229–45.

Krzywinska, T. (2008) 'Zombies in Gamespace: Form, Context, and Meaning in Zombie-Based Video Games', in McIntosh, S. and Leverette, M. (eds.) *Zombie Culture: Autopsies of the Living Dead*. Lanham, MD: Scarecrow Press, Inc., pp. 153–68.

Newbury, M. (2012) 'Fast Zombie/Slow Zombie: Food Writing, Horror Movies, and Agribusiness Apocalypse', *American Literary History*, 24(1), pp. 87–114. https://doi.org/10.1093/alh/ajr055

Pérez-Latorre, Ó. and Oliva, M. (2017) 'Video Games, Dystopia, and Neoliberalism: The Case of BioShock Infinite', *Games and Culture*, 14(7–8). pp. 781–800. https://doi.org/10.1177/1555412017727226

Puhl, R. M. and Heuer, C. A. (2009) 'The Stigma of Obesity: A Review and Update', *Obesity*, 17(5), pp. 941–64. https://doi.org/10.1038/oby.2008.636

Rothblum, E. D. (2012) 'Why a Journal on Fat Studies?', *Fat Studies*, 1(1), pp. 3–5. https://doi.org/10.1080/21604851.2012.633469

Sandlin, J. A. and Maudlin, J. G. (2012) 'Consuming Pedagogies: Controlling Images of Women as Consumers in Popular Culture', *Journal of Consumer Culture*, 12(2), pp. 175–94. https://doi.org/10.1177/1469540512446877

Schröter, F. and Thon, J-N. (2014) 'Video Game Characters: Theory and Analysis', *Diegesis*, 3(1), pp. 40–77. Available at: https://d-nb.info/1051788730/34 (Accessed: 11 December 2023).

Sherry, J. (1987) 'Four Modes of Caricature: Reflections upon a Genre', *Bulletin of Research in the Humanities*, pp. 1–42. Available at: https://jim-sherry.com/caricature.pdf (Accessed: 11 December 2023).

Sublette, C. M. (2016) 'The Last Twinkie in the Universe: Culinary Hedonism and Nostalgia in Zombie Films', in Sublette, C. M. and Martin, J. (eds.) *Devouring Cultures: Perspectives on Food, Power, and Identity from the Zombie Apocalypse to Downton Abbey*. Fayetteville: University of Arkansas Press, pp. 190–205.

Villoria, G. (2006) 'Keiji Inafune Interview', *GameSpy*, 21 February. Available at: https://xbox360.gamespy.com/xbox-360/dead-rising/690415p1.html (Accessed: 02 December 2023).

Weise, M. (2009) 'The Rules of Horror: Procedural Adaptation in Clock Tower, Resident Evil, and Dead Rising', in Perron, B. (ed.) *Horror Video Games: Essays on the Fusion of Fear and Play*. Jefferson, NC: McFarland, pp. 238–66.

5 Auditory Satire

Video game audio can satirise concepts, people, and the player's actions. When this occurs, a mode of videoludic satire called *auditory satire* is expressed. This mode of videoludic satire can be examined using methods of video game analysis proposed by Summers (2016). First, the researcher must partake in *analytical play* (Summers, 2016: 34), wherein they play the video game they are studying with the aim of discovering when and how sounds can be triggered or altered. Second, once the researcher is aware of the array of sounds present within their object of study, they should subject these sounds to a *topic analysis* (Summers, 2016: 40). In other words, they should conduct a semiotic reading of the sounds they have found within their object of study. Topic analyses are crucial to readings of auditory satire because they acknowledge that sound in video games "does not exist in a musically sealed world [and instead] draws upon a common musical lexicon from broader culture" (Summers, 2016: 40). Thereby, using these methods the signification of video game sounds can be read, allowing researchers to connect these sounds to wider concepts and reveal their aptitude for satirical criticism.

This chapter utilises notions of video game sound proposed by Collins (2008: 125) to describe how auditory satire appears in video games. Primarily, it draws on the concepts of *dynamic audio* and *non-dynamic audio*. Dynamic audio describes sound that responds to changes in the game state or actions enacted by the player. This type of audio can be divided into two modes. The first is *adaptive audio*, which is cued by the game-system under certain circumstances (this includes temporally and geographically situated music). The second is *interactive audio*, which is triggered by the player as a direct result of their physical input (pressing a button or moving a joystick, for example). Alternatively, non-dynamic audio describes game audio that cannot be impacted by the player, such as cutscene music. Of course, as Collins points out, such audio can be interrupted on an extra-diegetic level by players who reset or exit a game. Although, it remains true that the player is unable to influence non-dynamic audio while playing the game in the proper sense. Following these distinctions, the chapter introduces two categories of auditory satire: *dynamic auditory satire* and *non-dynamic auditory satire*. The former

DOI: 10.4324/9781003467175-6

category is also further divided further into *(adaptive) dynamic auditory satire* and *(interactive) dynamic auditory satire*.

Collins' terms are used to categorise auditory satire because they stress the uniqueness of sound in video games. Markedly, her terms are distinct from notions of sound in other audio-visual media, such as film, wherein sound is typically considered *diegetic* or *non-diegetic* depending on whether it exists as part of the world presented onscreen. These terms are not useful in conceptualising auditory satire, though,[1] especially as some sounds in video games can be classed as *transdiegetic* (Jørgensen, 2007). This term describes non-diegetic sound that can influence actions and events that take place inside a gameworld. For instance, in *Dead Rising 1* heavy metal music is triggered when the player's avatar reaches close proximity to a Psychopath. This music cannot be heard by the avatar, but it nonetheless influences their actions as the player is granted the knowledge of a substantial threat. When this occurs, a fight or flight response in the player is compelled by the audio, evidencing what Whalen refers to as an auditory "safety state/danger state binary" (2004: n.p.). Hence, the distinction between diegetic and non-diegetic sound is not only unstable, but also at times unsustainable when it comes to the impact each can have on a game's world.

This chapter is divided into three sections that exemplify and explore each form of auditory satire. In the first section on (adaptive) dynamic auditory satire, muzak[2] in *Dead Rising 1* and *2* is examined due to its association with both pacification and zombification. Respectively, these associations proceduralise a technique of satire expressed in Romero's *Dawn of the Dead* by lulling players into a (false) sense of security when gameplay is paused, only to violate this sense of security when gameplay resumes. In the second section on (interactive) dynamic auditory satire, in-game advertisements and collectible audio recordings in *Dead Rising 2* and *4* are examined for their satiric potential. Finally, in the third section, non-dynamic auditory satire is examined with reference to a song from *Dead Rising 4* called "Coldest Time of Year" (2016), which was written and produced by Oleksa Lozowchuk and performed by Melissa Kaplan. This song strengthens parallels made between the game's zombies and Black Friday shoppers. Overall, the chapter argues that auditory satire in *Dead Rising* games complements other forms of videoludic satire in these games (namely spatial and shared satire) by satirising excessive consumption and championing self-discipline.

(Adaptive) Dynamic Auditory Satire in *Dead Rising*

Background music in *Dead Rising* games does more than simply add ambience to their traversable environments; it contributes to their commentary on excessive consumption by producing (adaptive) dynamic auditory satire. This is made clear as background music featured in these games entangles notions of consumerism and zombiism to satirise the perceived preoccupation of U.S.

citizens (and the enacted preoccupation of the player) with consumer activities. Hence, an auditory parallel between *Dead Rising* games and Romero's *Dawn of the Dead* is evident, as in Romero's film "music and zombification are organically linked" (Carpenter, 2013: 1234). Yet, the auditory conflation of consumerism and zombiism in *Dead Rising* games is unique in that it relies on the player's input.

Carpenter summarises *Dawn of the Dead* succinctly when he describes the film as "a compelling if somewhat heavy-handed critique of contemporary American consumer culture" (2013: 1241) wherein zombies parody shoppers with their need to consume. But rather than focusing on the visual correlations between consumers and zombies, Carpenter examines their auditory connections. Crucially, he argues that muzak in *Dawn of the Dead* interweaves ideas of commercial spaces and zombies by signifying both simultaneously. To clarify, muzak in Romero's film (and elsewhere) signifies commercial spaces due to its general use as "an aural backdrop in [places] like offices, stores, and especially shopping malls" (2013: 1231). Moreover, muzak in *Dawn of the Dead* satirically embodies the undead due to its liminality: in a similar way that zombies occupy a liminal position between life and death, muzak in this film occupies a liminal position between diegetic and non-diegetic sound. This is most prominently displayed in the silly-sounding tune "The Gonk" (Herbert Chappell, 1965), which plays as the undead ravage the mall, as Stephen transforms into a zombie, and as the credits roll (Carpenter, 2013: 1244). Likewise, the satirical sentiment of muzak in *Dawn of the Dead* is reproduced in *Dead Rising* games. For example, in *Dead Rising 1* and *2* muzak is broadcast throughout the Willamette Parkview Mall and Fortune City. Although, it is more pronounced in areas of commerce. In *Dead Rising 2*'s Fortune Park, muzak can be difficult to hear (perhaps because this area is the central hub for the game's retail districts, rather than a retail district itself). Yet, in areas like the Royal Flush Plaza, muzak is clearly discernible. What is more, the moans of the undead can be heard alongside muzak in commercially driven locales. Consequently, an auditory link between consumerism and zombiism is established when players move their avatars directly into commercial spaces.

Audio in *Dead Rising 1* and *2* calls to mind an instance in *Dawn of the Dead* where The Gonk becomes infused with zombie groans after Stephen is bitten, dies, and reanimates as a zombie. In this scene, electronically generated zombie noises fuse with the ambient muzak, effectively zombifying the film's soundtrack: transforming it into "an aspect of the materiality of Romero's zombie horde" (Carpenter, 2013: 1245). After this, The Gonk is fragmented and distorted. Essentially, it becomes an auditory representation of the undead. However, muzak and the groans of the undead are often heard simultaneously in *Dead Rising 1* and *2*. Hence, while they can be understood as separate diegetic sounds, the prominence of both in the soundscape of these games fuses the two together. Because of this, the muzak in these games does not warrant an auditory transformation to be more explicitly perceived as zombie music; it is always recognisable as such. As such, the auditory satirisation of consumerism that is most palpable towards the end of Romero's film is present in *Dead Rising 1* and *2* from their onset.

As with spatial satire and shared satire in *Dead Rising* games, auditory satire promotes a sense of scepticism over commercially driven areas. In a literal sense, this is facilitated due to the audio's implied unsafety of these places. These are the domain of the undead, after all. But in a figurative sense, audio implies that consumer spaces are zombie spaces in their own right. This is especially apparent in *Dead Rising 1*, as there is little change in the volume of zombie groans when the player enters or exits shops (which the undead typically cluster outside of rather than within). Accordingly, zombie groans can be read as indicative of the avatar's proximity to consumer spaces rather than just their proximity to zombies. To some extent, this disrupts the idea that zombie groans are truly diegetic in this game; while these groans indicate a heavy presence of the undead, this is not always substantiated by the game's visuals. What is substantiated, though, is the idea that the avatar's entry into consumer spaces alludes to their (and the player's) symbolic entry into zombiism.

Auditory satire complements spatial satire on the false security of (post-9/11) consumerism in *Dead Rising 1* and *2* by suggesting that consumer spaces as unsafe. Also, in likening the avatar's physical entry into consumer spaces with their symbolic entry into zombiism, audio in *Dead Rising 1* and *2* conveys the message that such areas are predisposed to ensnare customers and transform them into allegorical slaves to consumerism. In this way, (adaptive) dynamic audio in these games embellishes instances of shared satire wherein the avatar is made to interact with agents that have succumbed to this fate, like Luz, Bessie, Rosa, and Erica as discussed in the previous chapter. Hence, by alluding to the zombifying pull of consumerism, the audio in these games cautions players against yielding to their consumer desires on a more abstract level. It signifies that the player should not engage in rampant consumption, as doing so cannot guarantee their avatar's safety and will only liken them with self-indulgent (and thereby not self-sufficient) video game agents.

As in *Dawn of the Dead*, muzak in *Dead Rising 1* evokes zombiism on its own terms due to its liminality – that is, its violation of the boundary between diegetic and non-diegetic sound. In *Dawn of the Dead*, the liminality of The Gonk is discernible as it can initially be interpreted as part of the film's score – as "analogous to the clumsy perambulations of the zombies" (Carpenter, 2013: 1244) – before being shown to come from the mall's speakers. Conversely, in *Dead Rising 1* the liminality of muzak is verified alongside player action; it can be heard when the player moves their avatar through gameplay environments (like the Paradise Plaza) and thereby appears to be part of the game's diegetic world. This is further emphasised due to the strict time constrains that dictate when muzak is played in *Dead Rising 1* (between the in-game hours of 10 a.m. and 10 p.m.). Although, if the player pauses the game by pressing the start button – suspending gameplay and prompting a menu screen to appear – muzak continues to play. Here, the sound transforms from a feature of the game's diegesis to an ambient sound that exists alongside the player's activity on a non-diegetic level. In addition, it is worth noting that while muzak continues to play as the game is paused, the groans of the undead cease.

As Whalen observes in the context of films, non-diegetic sound can function as "a kind of mediation between the space of the film and the audience" (2007: 71). The now non-diegetic background music in *Dead Rising 1* functions in a similar way. However, instead of underscoring dramatic events or character emotions, it works to incorporate the player into the game's satire on the false security of consumerism. With the muzak now isolated from the groans of the undead, it works to lull players into the very sense of security that the game critiques. As a standalone sound, the muzak here can function as it does in the real world: to establish "a mellow-yellow environment that brightens up one's days, recharges one's energies, alleviates stress, and calms frayed nerves" (Min, 2002).[3] Significantly, it can therefore operate as an *audioanalgesia*: a sound that diminishes the listener's capacity to "listen critically" (Lanza, cited in Min, 2002). This means that, when players pause *Dead Rising 1*, satirical effects may be encountered once they resume gameplay.

Players of *Dead Rising 1* may pause their game whilst battling the undead, forget what they were doing, and return to the game in a relaxed state only to be confronted by masses of zombies. Hence, the player can be lulled into a sense of security due to the calming sound of the game's muzak, only to have that security proven to be false, potentially quite jarringly, when they continue playing the game. In such an instance, pause menu muzak would adopt a counterintuitive, transdiegetic role. In other words, although this muzak appears to exist outside of the game's diegesis, it could still impact the events of the game's diegesis (negatively) if players failed to remember the immediacy of its undead threats. Thereby, pause menu muzak can allow for an effective proceduralisation of the satirical technique of *surprise*, whereby "[o]ne has been prepared to think along a certain channel and is trustfully proceeding on that path when [they are] abruptly switched to a totally unexpected direction" (Feinberg, 1967: 143). Likewise, even though *Dead Rising 2* and *4* have audio that is unique to their pause menus, this audio can still be categorised as muzak, meaning that the same scenario is possible with these games – on the contrary, *Dead Rising 2: OTR* and *3* use higher tempo music that is more action oriented than muzak and, as a result, sustains tension.

The potential violation of the player's sense of security after unpausing their game is alluded to by *Dead Rising 2*'s music composer/producer Oleksa Lozowchuk in an interview for Bloody Disgusting (Barkan, 2010). In this interview, Lozowchuk discusses the contrast in tone between the calming background music and violent gameplay of the second game. He even outlines a potential situation in which a player pauses the game to take a phone call before re-entering Fortune City in a soothed state due to the audio featured in the pause menu. Lozowchuk describes this audio as comically juxtaposed with the sounds of gameplay in *Dead Rising 2*, but it indicates much more than a humorous contrast. It indicates an opportunity for (adaptive) dynamic auditory satire to arise. In effect, dynamic audio in *Dead Rising* games can extend beyond the games themselves, permeating the space around players to implicate them directly in their satire on the false security of (post-9/11) consumption.

(Interactive) Dynamic Auditory Satire in *Dead Rising*

Dead Rising 4 expresses (interactive) dynamic auditory satire through in-game radios. These radios can be accessed if the avatar enters a car, wherein the player can direct them to toggle between two radio stations. One of these stations plays Christmas songs and the other plays country music.[4] Alternatively, the radio can be switched off by players who would prefer not to listen to it. Both radio stations make use of commercial breaks that foreground areas of commerce in the game's setting, Willamette. Due to the heavy presence of the undead in *Dead Rising 4*'s environments, these commercial breaks will inevitably be played alongside the sound of zombies groaning. As in the cases of (adaptive) dynamic auditory satire described above, the intertwining of sounds here once again conflates consumerism and zombiism, thereby satirising (and expressing scepticism towards) the former. However, while (adaptive) dynamic auditory satire in prior *Dead Rising* games is unavoidable as background music and zombie groans appear simultaneously as part of their landscapes, it is player determined when zombie groans are infused with radio ads in *Dead Rising 4*. As such, while both forms of dynamic auditory satire allude to *Dawn of the Dead*'s satirisation of consumer culture as described by Carpenter (2013), they accomplish this in distinct ways: with the former dictated by the game-system and the latter dictated by the player.

Even when separated from the sounds of the undead, radio ads in *Dead Rising 4* are satiric on their own terms. For instance, the radio ad for children's toy store, Toy Rex, indicates the Romeroean concept of a zombie consumer through its dialogue: "[growling] Life's a jungle – gym that is! When you look for the fun in everything you need an arsenal to match. Head to Toy Rex, the home for all adventurous kids. Toy Rex, where fun never goes extinct! [growling]." Presumably, the growling sounds that bookend this ad should signify Toy Rex's namesake, the Tyrannosaurus Rex. Yet, they sound remarkably like the growls emitted by zombies when the avatar is close to them. In fact, the player is likely to associate the growling sounds in this ad with the undead before registering that these sounds are implied to be the growls of a dinosaur. This is because the first growling sound in the ad for Toy Rex is decontextualised from its allusion to dinosaurs, making it more likely to conjure imagery of the undead when it is first heard – especially as the player will undoubtedly have heard the undead growling multiple times before encountering the radio ad.

Aside from conflating consumerism with zombiism, the radio ad for Toy Rex foregrounds *Dead Rising 4*'s satire on the false security of (post-9/11) consumerism. As Toy Rex can be visited by the avatar in the game, its radio ad sardonically hints at the defensive (or offensive) use of items held within the store by describing its wares in terms of an "arsenal." Here, auditory satire and spatial satire in *Dead Rising 4* work in conjunction to frame gameplay centred on excessive consumption as problematic. The former does this by sardonically marketing toys as defensive items and the latter does this by simulating the general ineffectualness of commodities in the face of a national crisis. This dissonance between the auditory marketing of goods and the reality of their fruitless consumption has the potential to enhance the idea that consumers are cultural dupes: an idea that is prominently expressed in shared satire in *Dead Rising* games. For instance, should players of *Dead Rising 4* venture into Toy Rex in search of an "arsenal" fit for combatting the game's undead enemies, they will be sorely disappointed by the items they can obtain there. Among these items is a toy laser sword, a toy hammer, and a toy gun – all of which are as weak as they are fragile. So, the (interactive) dynamic auditory satire expressed in the dialogue of the radio ad for Toy Rex has the potential to make a dupe of the player if this dialogue is taken at face value.

Sounds that stem from the avatar's use of toys found inside Toy Rex further reinforce *Dead Rising 4*'s spatial satire on excessive consumption. These sounds work to expose the false security of consumerism by arising from the player's decision to partake in ill-considered virtual consumption. Should the player direct their avatar to grab the magic wand toy on the back shelf of Toy Rex and use this item as a weapon, a twinkling sound will be triggered. Likewise, if the avatar is made to fire the toy gun obtained in the store, a light clicking sound will occur as a beanbag springs forth from the item. These sounds are *anempathetic*, meaning that they "exhibit conspicuous indifference to the situation" (Chion, 1994: 8). The sounds thereby highlight the absurdity of the player electing to utilise toys in their fight against the undead by complementing *Dead Rising 4*'s affordance-based spatial satire. That is to say, the sounds that these items make emphasise the physical ineffectiveness of toys during times of crisis. This is especially true given the contrast of these sounds with those of more combat-efficient items in the game. For example, machetes emit a visceral, slicing sound when used against in-game enemies, while assault rifles emit loud bangs. Thus, flimsy items make flimsy sounds, and flimsy sounds emphasise the folly of the player's inconspicuous virtual consumption while simultaneously encouraging rational consumption.

Radio ads and items in *Dead Rising 4* express (interactive) dynamic auditory satire that targets excessive consumption in a general sense. However, audio recordings scattered throughout the Willamette Memorial Megaplex and its surrounding areas add nuance to this satire by targeting the excesses of Black Friday in particular. Once players find these recordings, they can be accessed and played via *Dead Rising 4*'s pause menu. Once played, it becomes clear that these recordings offer exaggerated and parodic depictions of Black Friday shoppers. For Feinberg, a subject of parody "must have sufficient individuality of style or content to be distinguished" (1967: 184). This is true of Black Friday shoppers, who are recognisable in *Dead Rising 4*'s audio recordings not only because of their verbalised intent to attend Black Friday sales, but also by their acquisitiveness and violence. Hence, depictions of Black Friday shoppers in *Dead Rising 4*'s audio recordings align with the stereotypically hostile and commodity-obsessed vision of Black Friday shoppers in the popular cultural imagination. Attesting to this, news reports regularly relish the unruly scenes prompted by these shoppers, who have been branded "frantic, frenzied, upset, frustrated, angry, and crazy" (Lennon et al., 2018: 73).[5]

Black Friday shoppers are depicted as having an acquisitive nature in one of supporting character and amateur journalist Vick Chu's cloud uploads, which can be discovered by accessing portable hard drives throughout Willamette. In this recording, Vick interviews an unnamed survivor, who recalls an abnormal zombie with a deafening roar. However, before detailing her experience with the monster, the survivor provides some expositional titbits of information:

> Alright, uh… we were in line at the front entrance – we'd been in line for three days. My husband wanted the seventy-five inch TV from Foro-4 – I wanted the sushi set from Ripper's Knives. It was like 5am… and then, without any warning, people started screaming.
>
> (*Dead Rising 4*, 2016)

What is notable in this dialogue is the survivor's unprovoked mentioning of her consumer goals. The conversation could have easily, and more efficiently, occurred like this: "we were in line at the front entrance […] and then, without any warning, people started screaming." Instead, the survivor makes sure to mention her and her husband's purchasing plans, detailing specific shop names and desirable items. Considering that the outbreak had been occurring for six weeks by the time this interview took place, and that the crux of the survivor's story involves an abnormal creature attacking people, it is telling of her acquisitiveness that she remembers what her and her partner were hoping to buy. Moreover, an audio recording reduces Black Friday shoppers to squabbling, spoiled brats in one of Willamette's Personal Mysteries (collectible pieces of information that add story context to the game's world).[6] This recording features several shoppers arguing over a flat-screen television. A man and a woman compete for the item ("I was here first!", "No, I was!"), while another man loses his patience having been caught in the crossfire ("if either of you step on me again…").

The aforementioned audio recordings portray Black Friday shoppers as unable to exercise self-restraint, like out-of-control shoppers Bessie, Rosa, and Erica. Having been specifically asked to discuss an abnormal zombie, the woman in Vick's recording simply could not resist talking about shopping. Likewise, the shoppers arguing over the television appear on the brink of physical altercation. With these parodic depictions of Black Friday shoppers, *Dead Rising 4* legitimises a neoliberal rationality that privileges disciplined behaviour. As in instances of shared satire, this is achieved through notions of "ought" and "ought not." Namely, the woman in Vick's recording "ought" to be able to regulate her consumer desires by not reminiscing over them in a way that is tangential to Vick's questioning. Additionally, she "ought not" to be so preoccupied with acquisitive behaviour, as evidenced by her inability to avoid mentioning consumer goods. Furthermore, the squabbling shoppers "ought" to behave in a respectable manner and "ought not" to require the disciplining of a mall security worker ("Back off, or I am removing all three of you from line and we'll see who gets a flat-inch TV then. Understood?"). Notions of self-control and restraint are thereby legitimised through audio-based condemnations of the unchecked acquisitiveness and emotional outbursts of Black Friday shoppers in *Dead Rising 4*.

Non-dynamic Auditory Satire in *Dead Rising*

Non-dynamic audio is typically bound to a game's "introductory movies and cinematics" (Collins, 2008: 125). As a result, players cannot usually alter the placement of non-dynamic audio; they cannot move a character's conversation from one cutscene to the next, for example. Players might be able to impact the delivery of non-dynamic audio though, with some games making this possible via their settings. For instance, players may be able to toggle the volume of in-game sounds, perhaps lowering a cutscene's ambient sound and raising the sound of dialogue. In this way, the player does not have an impact over what sounds are played, though they could customise the delivery of such sounds. However, despite the disassociation between non-dynamic audio and gameplay, this type of audio still has the potential to influence how players perceive and navigate gameworlds.

As with some of the examples of dynamic auditory satire detailed above, non-dynamic auditory satire can be considered transdiegetic. This is evident in *Dead Rising 4* with regards to the song "Coldest Time of Year" (2016),[7] which plays during a cutscene depicting the opening of the Willamette Memorial Megaplex on the day of the Black Friday sales. In this cutscene, Black Friday shoppers cluster at the entrance to Willamette's newest retail hub, run rampant within it, and fight over toys before transforming into zombies: allegorical figures representing and satirising the drive of U.S. citizens towards materialistic consumption. Significantly, "Coldest Time of Year" mirrors this transformation, auditorily conflating notions of consumerism with zombiism in a way that synchronises with the visualisation of the mall's downfall. Hence, the song is *empathetic* (Chion, 1994: 8) in that it works in conjunction with what is happening onscreen to produce its satiric meaning.

Initially, "Coldest Time of Year" seems like a faithful rendition of "O Christmas Tree"[8] as lines from the latter song are reproduced as the virtual camera moves towards a small, seasonally decorated shop. Then, a shift occurs as the titular lyrics are added. Tellingly of the game's satire, this happens alongside a shot transition which moves the focus from the shop to a news reporter publicising the opening of the Willamette Memorial Megaplex – the largest mall in the world, according to a news banner. Then, the titular lyrics are vocalised again alongside an establishing shot of the Willamette Memorial Megaplex's entrance: this leads into shots of a decorative banner announcing the Black Friday sales, a crowd banging on the mall's doors, and a pair of shoppers fighting over a teddy bear (Figure 5.1). From a literal standpoint, these lyrics reference the climate. After all, Black Friday occurs annually on the fourth Friday of November – on the cusp of Winter in the Northern Hemisphere. Attesting to this, the cutscene visualises seasonal chilliness with snow and people wearing thick coats. However, when read against the backdrop of sale signs, restless crowds, and squabbling shoppers, these lyrics take on an alternate meaning.

Lozowchuk's "Coldest Time of Year" signifies a distinct lack of affection: emotional coldness that correlates with shoppers violently seeking material goods during the Black Friday sales. Furthermore, the song's conflation of cold-heartedness and unchecked consumption evokes a common assumption about the holiday period. As Miller explains, it is often supposed that "Christmas was once indeed the pure festival of close family togetherness, but its heart

Figure 5.1 Shoppers fighting over a teddy bear before the zombie outbreak in *Dead Rising 4*.

has been lost in the relentless exploitation of its possibilities by a combination of individual materialism and capitalist profit-taking" (2017: 429). Enforcing this viewpoint, *Dead Rising 4* rejects notions of the Christmas season as a period of familial warmth and togetherness in favour of presenting it as one that has been usurped by capitalism and excessive consumer spending. In turn, it satirises these values by equating superfluous seasonal shopping with selfishness and, by extension, the mindless violence of rabid zombies.

Melissa Kaplan's vocal performance strengthens the non-dynamic auditory satire of "Coldest Time of Year" with its evocation of zombiism. Accordingly, this song can be thought of as *Dead Rising 4*'s version of The Gonk from *Dawn of the Dead.* As pointed out earlier with regards to this film, The Gonk undergoes a transformation when Stephen dies; it alters "as electronically-generated moans merge with the track, which then starts to blur and distort" (Carpenter, 2013: 1244). Proceeding this, the zombie-infused sound of the music leads into a shot revealing a newly zombified Stephen. The Gonk, having transformed alongside the filmic protagonist, "then attempts, but fails to re-establish itself, and falls to pieces in clattering, echoing fragments as Stephen's misshapen corpse stumbles away" (Carpenter, 2013: 1244). Likewise, in *Dead Rising 4*, "Coldest Time of Year" transforms from a solemnly performed Christmas song into an auditory signifier of zombification as a woman and man fight over a teddy bear and the occupants of the Willamette Memorial Megaplex turn into zombies.

With regards to The Gonk, allusions to zombiism are achieved due to the fragmentary mismatch of zombie groans and muzak: a distortion of the musical score that sees the altered tune "limping along as if in sympathy with the undead" (Carpenter, 2013: 1245). With "Coldest Time of Year" a similar effect transpires through Kaplan's performance. During the fall of the Willamette Memorial Megaplex, the song once more repeats lyrics from "O Christmas Tree." This time, though, these lyrics are fragmented, merely echoing those reproduced at the beginning of the song; this fragmentation is apparent in Kaplan's staggard delivery of the lines, in which she emphasises each syllable. Combined with the discernibly lower pitch of Kaplan's voice and the almost five-second delay between the second-to-last and last words of the song, this mode of delivery adds a zombie like quality to the music. It suggests a level of forgetfulness – of losing one's mind. Thus, "Coldest Time of Year" does not just call to mind the undead by working in tandem with the onscreen image; it also manages to do so through Kaplan's vocal performance.

Rather than merely cautioning against the zombifying effects of consumerism, as *Dawn of the Dead* does, *Dead Rising* games allow players to choose between partaking in or avoiding simulating consumer behaviour. Thus, "Coldest Time of Year" can be read as a warning to players against adopting a consumer-oriented gameplay style. In *Dead Rising 4*, this behaviour may include gathering a multitude of Christmas-related items: such as holiday bells, ornaments (baubles), and shopping valuables, the latter or which are stylised as a pile of Christmas presents in this game. Much like the items discussed in the chapter on spatial satire, these trinkets are of marginal use against the game's relentless zombie hordes. Hence, the implications of "Coldest Time of Year" can carry over to the player's gaming experience. Consequently, the song exists in tandem with the game's spatial and shared satire, as a means of promoting self-control by satirising uninhibited consumption.

Conclusion

Video game audio can satirise concepts, people, and player actions. In *Dead Rising* games, this is made apparent as auditory satire targets excessive consumption, seasonal shoppers, and retail-oriented player actions. Dynamic audio in *Dead Rising* games depict consumers as materialistic dupes by way of ambient sounds, audio recordings, and combat-related noises. Crucially, with the latter, materialistic gameplay is undermined by the sounds in-game items can make, not just their minimalistic/limited affordances (as described in the previous chapter's examples of spatial satire). Moreover, non-dynamic audio in *Dead Rising 4* rejects notions of the Christmas period as one facilitating human warmth and togetherness. Instead, the season is satirically posited as the "Coldest Time of Year" due to its emphasis on excessive commercialism.

From an ideological perspective, analyses of auditory satire in *Dead Rising* games show that these games legitimise the ideal of self-discipline while condemning excessive consumption. Auditory satire in these games, then, complements their spatial satire and shared satire. What is more, satirical sounds that occur because of the player's actions in *Dead Rising* games foreground the potential for video games to satirise their own players. Indeed, audio serves as both a warning against and a criticism of the player's engagement in excessive consumption in *Dead Rising* games. Yet, sound is not the only means by which such warnings and criticism are conveyed, as the following chapter on temporal satire demonstrates.

Notes

1 The distinction between diegetic and non-diegetic sound can even be challenged across audio-visual media texts, which can, of course, construct their own communicative logic. Therefore, it is not a requirement for texts to maintain a clear division between these sounds (Jørgensen, 2017).

2 This term refers to "piped-in, easy-listening, lightly-orchestrated pop tunes" (Carpenter, 2013: 1231) that are typically played in public spaces.

3 Similarly, both Eno (1978) and Jones and Shumacher (1992: 161) claim that muzak is calming.

4 The latter radio station again situates the game's satire in an American context.

5 For example, the British news outlet *The Guardian* published an article titled "Black Friday spawns chaotic scenes as America goes wild in the aisles" (Williams, 2012). Here, it is revealed that one customer abandoned his girlfriend's child to look for a television while another customer threatened somebody with a gun. Furthermore,

several deaths by shooting were reported in the U.S. during 2016 alone: the year *Dead Rising 4* was released (Weill, 2016; Kaplan, 2020).

6 The Personal Mystery in question is called "Blackest Friday."

7 The title of "Coldest Time of Year" also alludes to and subverts the popular Christmas song, "It's the Most Wonderful Time of the Year" (1963).

8 This song has been translated (with multiple variations) from the German "O Tannenbaum," which was written by Ernst Anschütz in 1824.

References

Barkan, J. (2010) 'Exclusive Interview: Composer Oleksa Lozowchuk "Dead Rising 2"', *Bloody Disgusting*, 28 September. Available at: https://bloody-disgusting.com/news/119723/exclusive-interview-composer-oleksa-lozowchuk-dead-rising-2/ (Accessed: 12 December 2023).

Carpenter, A. (2013) 'Dead in Tune: Uncanny Muzak® in Dawn of the Dead', *The Journal of Popular Culture*, 46(6), pp. 1231–52. https://doi.org/10.1111/jpcu.12086

Chion, M. (1994) *Audio vision: Sound on Screen*. New York: Columbia University Press.

Collins, K. (2008) *Game Sound: An Introduction to the History, Theory, and Practice of Video Game Music and Sound Design*. Cambridge, MA: MIT Press.

Eno, B. (1978) Music for Airports / Ambient 1 [Liner Notes]. Available at: https://www.bussigel.com/technosonics/wordpress/wp-content/uploads/2016/07/eno-ambient.pdf (Accessed 07 August 2021).

Feinberg, L. (1967) *Introduction to Satire*. Reprint 2008. Santa Fe, NM: Pilgrims Process, Inc.

Jones, S. C. and Shumacher, T. G. (1992) 'Muzak: On Functional Music and Power', *Critical Studies in Mass Communication*, 9(2), pp. 156–69. https://doi.org/10.1080/15295039209366822

Jørgensen, K. (2007) *What are Those Grunts and Growls Over There?* PhD thesis, Copenhagen University. Available at: https://citeseerx.ist.psu.edu/document?repid=rep1&type=pdf&doi=a8c794853c33e8182dbe9c7152b09e9c59a9f44a (Accessed: 13 December 2023).

Jørgensen, K. (2017) 'Emphatic and Ecological Sounds in Gameworld Interfaces', in Mera, M., Sadoff, R. and Winters, B. (eds.) *The Routledge Companion to Screen Music and Sound*. London: Routledge, pp. 72–84.

Kaplan, M. (2020) 'Black Friday's Most Gruesome Injuries and Deaths through the Years', *The New York Post*, 27 November. Available at: https://nypost.com/article/black-fridays-most-gruesome-injuries-and-deaths-through-the-years/ (Accessed 27 June 2024).

Lennon, S. J., Kim, M., Lee, J. and Johnson, K. K. P. (2018) 'Consumer Emotions on Black Friday: Antecedents and Consequence', *Journal of Research for Consumers*, 32(1), pp. 70–109. Available at: https://jrconsumers.com/Academic_Articles/issue_32/Issue32-AcademicArticle-Kim70-109.pdf (Accessed: 12 December 2023).

Miller, D. (2017) 'Christmas: An anthropological lens', *Hau: Journal of* Ethnographic *Theory*, 7(3), pp. 409–442. https://doi.org/10.14318/hau7.3.027

Min, S. (2002) 'Soothe Operator: Muzak and Modern Sound Art', *Cabinet*, Summer. Available at: https://www.cabinetmagazine.org/issues/7/min.php (Accessed: 13 December 2023).

Summers, T. (2016) *Understanding Video Game Music*. Cambridge: Cambridge University Press.

Weill, J. (2016) 'Black Friday 2016 Turns Deadly in Multiple Shootings at Malls', *The Daily Beast*, 25 November. Available from: https://www.thedailybeast.com/black-friday-2016-turns-deadly-in-multiple-shootings-at-malls (Accessed 27 June 2024).

Whalen, Z. (2004) 'Play Along – An Approach to Videogame Music', *Game Studies*, 4(1), Available from: https://gamestudies.org/0401/whalen/ (Accessed: 13 December 2023).

Whalen, Z. (2007) 'Case Study: Film Music Vs. Video Game Music: The Case of Silent Hill', in Sexton, J. (ed.). *Music, Sound and Multimedia: From the Live to the Virtual*. Edinburgh: Edinburgh University Press, pp. 68–81.

Williams, M. (2012) 'Black Friday Spawns Chaotic Scenes as America Goes Wild in the Aisles', *The Guardian*, 23 November. Available from: https://www.theguardian.com/world/us-news-blog/2012/nov/23/black-friday-chaos-america (Accessed 23 January 2020).

6 Temporal Satire

Temporal satire occurs when video games emphasise the passage of time for the purpose of satire. Accordingly, a player's (mis)use of time in video games can be read as satirical by way of qualitative content analysis. That is, by exploring the implications inherent in the ways video games contextualise the player's temporal investments in gameplay activities. Temporal satire can be conceptualised using Caillois' (1961: 13) *ludus* and *paidia* continuum, which separates games and play by structural depth. As explained by Caillois, chess has a rigid rule set and so conforms to the expectations of ludus, whereas children whirling around in circles with no other aim than to produce a fanciful sense of enjoyment encapsulates paidia (1961: 13). Correspondingly, temporal satire can manifest as *ludus-based temporal satire* or *paidia-based temporal satire*. The former describes temporal satire stemming from the player's engagement in structured (if not monotonous) gameplay activities with the aim of fulfilling objectives. The latter describes temporal satire resulting from the player's engagement in freeform gameplay that rejects the pursuit of such objectives.

The concepts of ludus and paidia are not used uncritically to conceptualise the forms of temporal satire. This is because the use of these terms by Caillois preceded the development and subsequent popularisation of video games. Moreover, the inherent codification of video games complicates Caillois' continuum. As Newman asserts, despite "how creative, exploratory, resistant, or deviant the player's performance might be, it *is* bounded by rules [emphasis in original]" (2013: 102). In other words, as technological artefacts, the intrinsic rules of video games ensure that even the most whimsical of activities facilitated by these games are algorithmically determined. But rather than dismissing ludus and paidia as conceptually irrelevant to video games, this chapter adopts Frasca's definitional revisions of Caillois' terms. For Frasca (2001: 7–10), ludus encompasses gameplay activities that lead to the delineation of winners and losers (or promote gains and losses), whereas paidia does not. Concerning paidia, the player's physical and cognitive endeavours during gameplay serve experiential enjoyment exclusively. So, with Frasca's added nuance, ludus and paidia continue to encapsulate Caillois' partition

DOI: 10.4324/9781003467175-7

between regulated and spontaneous behaviour in such a way that better suits their application to video games.

Temporal satire is signalled by the foregrounding of time in video games. Hence, the first step in recognising temporal satire is to determine whether a video game places an emphasis on time. One way of doing this is by examining what Malliet refers to as a game's *elements of representation* (2007). That is, their visual and narrative properties: in-game items, day/night transitions, thematic elements, and character conversations, for instance. Likewise, Consalvo and Dutton's *interface study* (2006) method of gameplay analysis can be used to determine the presence of temporal satire. This involves the examination of a range of on-screen information, such as that detailing

> the life, health, location or status of the character(s), as well as battle or action menus, nested menus that control options such as advancement grids or weapons selections, or additional screens that give the player more control over manipulating elements of gameplay.
>
> (Consalvo and Dutton, 2006)

Although, in the context of discerning temporal satire, only information pertaining to the passage of time needs to be searched for, such as clocks, timers, or other references to temporality. Once an emphasis on the passage of time in a video game has been established, readings of gameplay activities in relation to this can commence and temporal satire can be perceived.

In *Dead Rising* games, temporal satire targeting excessive consumption manifests when players engage in "consumption play" (Lehdonvitta et al., 2009: 1061). This style of gameplay centres on the acquisition of virtual commodities and, in *Dead Rising* games, has the potential to detract from transient story missions, which these games prioritise above all else. Consequently, consumption play is often contextualised as counterproductive in *Dead Rising* games; it is a waste of time that could be better spent in pursuit of knowledge and self-preservation. Thus, players engaging with this gameplay style are framed as objects of satire. Evidencing this, the following five sections work towards conceptualising temporal satire further and examining its manifestations in *Dead Rising* games. In the first section, theorisations of time in video games are explored to verify how time spent engaging in gameplay activities can be perceived as wasteful. Then, in the second section, the foregrounding of time in *Dead Rising* games is evidenced via examinations of their elements of representation and their interfaces. Following this, the third section presents a more detailed account of consumption play and explains its significance in *Dead Rising* games. Finally, the fourth and fifth sections demonstrate how *Dead Rising* games provide ludus and paidia-based avenues for players to engage in consumption play, while satirising players who prioritise this mode of gameplay over story progression.

Time in Video Games

Scholars typically approach time in video games from one of two perspectives: formalist or experiential. The former "sees time evolving in a reference between the game state and play time" whereas the latter "tries to describe a player's comprehension of temporal situations in games" (Nitsche, 2007: 145–6). Therefore, formalist approaches to time in video games aim to classify the varying temporalities players are subject to, as well point to ways in which these temporalities can be manipulated or interrupted. Alternatively, experiential approaches aim to describe how players perceive (or are invited to perceive) the passage of time within a game. By exploring how a player's expenditure of time can be contextualised as satirical by a game system, temporal satire is primarily an experiential phenomenon. Yet, to describe temporal satire, terminology concerning formalist ideas on video game temporalities is necessarily utilised. Accordingly, relevant facets of formalist and experiential approaches to time in video games are detailed below.

Illustrative of formalist concepts regarding video game temporalities are Juul's (2005) *play time* and *fictional time*. These terms describe the time it takes for the player to play a game and the time it takes for events to happen in the world of said game. Play time and fictional time can occur on a 1:1 basis, meaning that the progression of time in a game is synchronous with the progression of time in the real world.[1] Additionally, the relationship between play time and fictional time may be asynchronous, as it is in *Dead Rising* games. These games typically adopt a temporal structure that sees time in their worlds progress more quickly than time in the real world, with one minute of in-game time equating to roughly five seconds of real time – this can be said of *Dead Rising 1*, *2*, *2: Off The Record*, and *3* (on its standard difficulty setting).[2] Temporal satire arises from the player's experiences of *play time* and *fictional time*. In the above mentioned *Dead Rising* games, it can stem from the player's consumption-oriented temporal investments in play/fictional time, which are depicted as unnecessary or otherwise unimportant. As such, temporal satire in *Dead Rising* games is made apparent by their allowance for, and the player's participation in, what these games contextualise as *wasted time*.[3]

Wasted time can be likened to Juul's *dead time* in the sense that both involve the player's participation in trivial activities. As an experiential concept regarding video game temporalities, dead time describes time lost to players engaging in "unchallenging activities for the sake of a higher goal" (Juul, 2004: 138). For example, in massively multiplayer online role-playing games this might include "spend[ing] hours or days doing mundane tasks such as walking, waiting for monsters to respawn, or even fishing or chopping wood" (Juul, 2005: 155–6). Such tasks are essential to gameplay progression, but they do not always inspire the interest of players. Hence, dead time serves as a temporal measurement of the player's efforts to attain game goals at the cost of their enjoyment. Yet, wasted time is less subjective than dead time in that it does not require researchers to make a value judgement on whether it is "dull" or "hold[s] no interest [for players]" (Juul, 2005: 156). Indeed, consumption-oriented gameplay activities can certainly be enjoyable for players of *Dead Rising* games, though these activities still initiate wasted time due to their detraction from the games' story-based objectives. As such, this chapter does not claim that wasted time is not subjective at all, but rather it asserts that wasted time is not subjective from the point of view of the researcher, who must discern what a game's developers have delineated as wasted time. To reiterate, wasted time describes time spent by players on gameplay activities that are portrayed as unimportant, rather than time spent on gameplay activities that a researcher considers boring.

Time in *Dead Rising* Games

Dead Rising games repeatedly emphasise the passage of time with their timer systems, which see fictional time in *Dead Rising 1*, *2*, *2: Off The Record*, and *3* progress alongside play time, albeit at a much faster rate. In these games, gameplay opportunities adhere to a strict time schedule. That is, they are only available at certain in-game times. For instance, the first story mission in *Dead Rising 1* commences from 12:00 p.m. on the 19th of September (Frank's first day in the Willamette Parkview Mall). If this mission is not completed by 5 p.m. on the same day, it will expire. In addition, players will not be able to start subsequent story missions, which require the completion of former ones. Consequently, Frank will not discover the truth behind the zombie outbreak in Willamette and the player will not unlock the game's canonical ending. As such, time management is essential for players to progress through this game's story and reach its true resolution. Likewise, the player must manage their time well to complete the story missions of *Dead Rising 2*, *2: Off The Record*, and *3* to discover the cause of each game's respective zombie outbreak and unlock their canonical endings.

Visually, time is alluded to in *Dead Rising* games via clocks. These items do not dominate the environments in these games. However, they do appear in places where the player is likely to traverse, such as near passageways between gameplay areas or in places that the player must explore to fulfil story objectives. For example, in *Dead Rising 1* an ornamental structure featuring a clock is displayed in the Paradise Plaza and a 12-hour striking clock can be found (and heard) in the central Leisure Park. The first of these clocks is situated next to a door that leads to the mall's security room, and so will be passed several times if the player chooses to save survivors. The second clock is attached to a tower that the avatar must climb inside towards the end of the game. Avatars in *Dead Rising 1*, *2*, and *2: Off The Record* also wear watches that can be examined by players, enabling them to keep track of fictional times and tasks (Figure 6.1). In *Dead Rising 3*, the time of day is visible on the pause menu alongside details of the player's objectives.

Figure 6.1 Chuck examines his watch in *Dead Rising 2*.

Dead Rising games use narrative information and aspects of their interfaces to infer that story missions should be the main priority for players. This inference is achieved by cutscenes containing narrative exposition, which stresses the stringent time frames available in each game: Frank has three days to uncover the truth of the outbreak before a rescue helicopter arrives in *Dead Rising 1*; Chuck and Frank have three days to escape Fortune City before it is firebombed in *Dead Rising 2* and *2: Off The Record*; Nick has six days to fix an aeroplane and escape Los Perdidos before it is bombed in *Dead Rising 3*. Furthermore, on-screen bars signify the limited availability of objectives pertaining to each game's story. In *Dead Rising 1*, *2*, and *2: Off The Record*, these bars are either long and blue (indicating that more than six in-game hours are available), medium and yellow (indicating that less than six in-game hours are available), or short and red (indicating that less than three in-game hours are available). In *Dead Rising 3*, the bars are all one colour (white) but continue to indicate the depletion of game time by decreasing in length.

Some tasks in *Dead Rising* games are inconsequential in the sense that their completion, or lack thereof, does not impact the avatar's discovery of the truth behind each game's zombie outbreak or their escape from Willamette, Fortune City, or Los Perdidos. An example of such tasks are side missions, which typically involve rescuing survivors and running errands, like finding and delivering items to people (as in the Restaurant Man, Bent Wood, and Shopping Spree side missions addressed in Chapter 4). As with story missions, side missions have on-screen bars signifying how much time the player has left to complete them. However, the bars for side missions are distinct from those linked to story missions. In *Dead Rising 1*, *2*, and *2: Off The Record*, this distinction is communicated via their placement on the game interface. Story missions are always placed at the top of the screen, with side missions falling beneath them. Similarly, in *Dead Rising 3*, story missions and side missions are placed in two separate boxes on the pause menu. As before, the former are situated above the latter. Thus, *Dead Rising* games present a hierarchical positioning in relation to their story missions and side missions that suggest to players that they should value story progression above all else. As such, time spent engaging in activities that do not progress each game's story (many of which are consumption related) can be thought of as wasted time.

Consumption Play in *Dead Rising*

With regards to consumption-oriented activities in video games, Molesworth and Denegri-Knott claim that "digital virtual spaces (stages) and virtual commodities (props) may encourage framed but unique performances that allow for an actualization (release through performance) of the desire built up by consumers' imaginations" (2007: 125). *Dead Rising* games accomplish this by enabling consumption play, and in doing so surpass Romero's *Dawn of the Dead* in terms of their ability to conjure consumer fantasies. For Loudermilk (2003), sequences of consumer delight in *Dawn of the Dead* constitute what he calls *Mall Fantasia*. This phenomenon describes the euphoric sensation experienced by the four protagonists of Romero's film after they take control of a mall and its material goods, as well as filmic audiences who live vicariously through them. Likewise, Briefel claims that notions of consumer pleasure in *Dawn of the Dead* reach their pinnacle via the implementation of what she calls a *Bliss Montage*: a sequence that "sets the characters' free-shopping escapades to lively extra-diegetic music" (2011: 144). Once more, this phenomenon describes a revelling in the joys of consumption by both the film's protagonists and viewers. Regarding *Dead Rising* games, the feelings of consumer delight conjured by Mall Fantasia and Bliss Montages can be replicated and enhanced as players *simulate* consumer pleasure, rather than simply enjoy the observation of such pleasure. Truly, Schott (2011: 147) determines that a major appeal of *Dead Rising 1* is the freedom to take items from the Willamette Parkview Mall: an appeal that extends to the game's sequels with their multitude of items in their respective locales.

In *Dead Rising* games, outlandish consumer fantasies are facilitated by gameworlds containing an abundance of freely accessibly consumer items. However, these fantasies cannot be actualised unconditionally. This is because they use up valuable fictional time that the visual and narrative information presented in *Dead Rising* games infer should be spent on completing story missions. Not only is this inferred by the length/colour changing bars foregrounding story missions, but also by the conspicuous lack of such bars in relation to other activities that players can partake in – activities that go beyond those of either story missions or side missions and stem from freeform gameplay. For instance, there are no interface related incentives to simply explore stores or try on every item of clothing in Willamette, Fortune City, or Los Perdidos. Thus, the player's temporal investments in such activities are satirised due to the contextualisation of these activities as wastes of time. Indeed, before Frank arrives at the Willamette Parkview Mall in *Dead Rising 1*, helicopter pilot Ed DeLuca remarks that "the only thing to do in [Willamette] is kill time at the shopping mall" – a comment that portrays consumerism as an idle activity. As such, temporal satire can manifest as players of *Dead Rising* games adopt the same sense of consumption-oriented comfort that is condemned by Fran in *Dawn of the Dead*; it can manifest as players of *Dead Rising* games become "hypnotized" by the allure of their settings.

Story missions in *Dead Rising* games centralise their avatars' vocational and parental responsibilities. In *Dead Rising 1* and *2: Off The Record* these missions revolve around Frank's journalistic pursuits, in *Dead Rising 2* they are driven by Chuck's drive to protect his daughter and prove that he did not cause the Fortune City outbreak (by assisting journalist Rebecca Chang uncover the cause of the outbreak for her news station), and in *Dead Rising 3* they intertwine with Nick's job as a mechanic (as he must locate machinery and build a plane to escape Los Perdidos). Significantly, these story missions are not available during every moment of gameplay and instead occur at varying intervals throughout the aforementioned games. This leaves gaps in the fictional times of *Dead Rising 1*, *2*, *2: Off The Record*, and *3* wherein the player can indulge in consumption play in a way that satisfies the neoliberal demand to "enjoy responsibly" (Bailes, 2019: 28). That is, in a way that does not hinder the player's progression through story missions. Hence, not all consumption play in *Dead Rising* games leads to a temporal satirisation of the player; temporal satire only occurs when consumption play eats into the fictional time that these games suggest should be spent on story missions. Thus, in line with neoliberal ideals, *Dead Rising* games satirise players who engage in *excessive* consumption play. In other words, they satirise players who engage in consumption play that disrupts the idealised balance between productivity and pleasure.

Ludus-based Temporal Satire

Adding to their primary objectives, which involve investigating and surviving zombie outbreaks, *Dead Rising* games provide players with a variety of secondary objectives in the form of video game achievements. These can be highlighted by menu screens, loading screens, or pop-up notifications inside video games. Alternatively, they can be described outside of these games via designated achievement areas: screens dedicated to "Trophies" or "Achievements" on PlayStation and Xbox consoles, for example. In *Dead Rising 1*, *2*, *2: Off The Record*, and *3*, the player's pursuit of achievements can give rise to wasted time. This is because achievements can serve as distractions from story missions and, due to the strict countdown clocks featured in these games, may even cause players to fail these missions. Because achievements have victory conditions (set tasks with the reward of a virtual trophy or Gamerscore), players who strive to attain them partake in ludus as Frasca (2001) reimagines it. Consequently, in *Dead Rising* games, ludus-based temporal satire can manifest as players dedicate their time to fulfilling the requirements of achievements rather than striving to complete time-sensitive story missions.

Many achievements in *Dead Rising* games focus on the collection and utilisation of in-game objects. As distractions from story missions, these achievements thereby facilitate the hypnosis that Fran spoke of when critiquing the fascination of her fellow survivors with the mall in *Dawn of the Dead*. Achievements in *Dead Rising* games can thereby facilitate what Loudermilk (2003: 93) calls "consumer dementia" – a term used to describe the preoccupation of survivors in *Dawn of the Dead* with commodities in their mall hideaway. This preoccupation takes the form of delirium when the protagonists of Romero's film rejoice in their newfound retail paradise and forget about the impending threat of the undead. Correspondingly, players of *Dead Rising* games can prioritise consumption play and disregard discovering the sources of, and escaping from, each game's zombie outbreak. In such instances, players themselves are framed as objects of satire by taking on the materialistic nature of characters like Luz, Bessie, Rosa, and Erica, as discussed in Chapter 4 on shared satire.

In a marked deviation from Romero's film, though, zombie threats in *Dead Rising* games are not so much forgotten by players as they are ignored by them. Truly, it would be difficult to forget about the threat of the undead with so many zombies present within these games. What is more, avatars are thrust into a near permanent state of closeness to zombies in *Dead Rising* games, unlike the protagonists of *Dawn of the Dead*. Therefore, in the context of *Dead Rising* games, Loudermilk's "consumer dementia" can be more accurately thought of as *consumer recklessness* – especially as it is more akin to Roger's irresponsible (and fatal) pursuit of a bag of tools that he dropped, rather than the idyllic exploits of Romero's ensemble after securing their consumer haven. Still, this only strengthens the pertinence of ludus-based temporal satire in *Dead Rising* games when players' preoccupations with consumption prevails despite the obvious dangers surrounding their avatars.

In *Dead Rising* games, consumption play is promoted by several retail-oriented achievements that focus on trying on clothes, visiting shops, and acquiring gifts. For example, *Dead Rising 1*'s Sharp Dresser achievement requires Frank to try on 20 different costumes. Accordingly, this achievement is prone to eating away at the game's precious fictional time, principally as stores in the Willamette Parkview Mall offer few clothing options despite displaying an array of outfits. Indeed, a men's apparel store called The Distinguished Gentleman visually showcases a variety of shirts, blazers, and trousers that are mostly unattainable. In total, there are four points of interaction within this store: two by the changing rooms and two by a shoe rack. Yet, these only grant two costume changing options. One gives Frank an outfit consisting of a fur trim coat, shirt and slacks, while the other gives him a pair of formal shoes. On top of that, clothing items can be duplicated in different stores, meaning that the player is likely to command Frank to change into the same outfit multiple times. Hence, the process of attaining the Sharp Dresser achievement can be incredibly longwinded.

More nuanced examples of ludus-based temporal satire occur in *Dead Rising 2*, with its Father of the Month and Father of the Year achievements. These task players with giving gifts to Chuck's daughter, Katey. One gift is required to attain the former achievement and 11 are needed to attain the latter one. Gifts mostly comprise of consumer items, like artwork, toys, and large stuffed animals – though a live tiger called Snowflake can also be gifted to Katey. These gifts can take some time to acquire, especially since Snowflake and the "funny painting" can only be obtained in specific side missions. To be exact, Snowflake can be recruited after the player tames her in a mission that starts at 4:00 a.m. on the first day of the outbreak and ends at 10:00 a.m. on its second day. Alternatively, the funny painting is obtained from a man named Randolph Allen in a mission that starts at 11:00 a.m. on the third day of the outbreak and ends at 7:00 p.m. on the same day.

Eight out of the eleven gifts for the Father of the Year achievement can be found in the Royal Flush Plaza, which is the area located immediately outside of the emergency shelter where Katey resides. However, five of these gifts (the giant stuffed bull, giant stuffed donkey, giant stuffed elephant, giant stuffed rabbit, and robot bear) cannot be stored in Chuck's inventory. Instead, they must be carried in the same fashion as the shopping valuables from the Shopping Spree side mission discussed in Chapter 4. To reiterate, these gifts always need to be held by Chuck; if he substitutes them for another item, they will fall to the ground rather than simply occupying an inventory slot. Ergo, just as Chuck sought to protect the shopping valuables in Shopping Spree so too must he protect these gifts for Katey, who will not accept damaged goods. As a result, Chuck must be made to traverse the Royal Flush Plaza on five separate occasions to obtain these unique gifts for his daughter – each time making sure not to damage them. If the gifts are damaged, Chuck will be required to acquire them again. Hence, it is easy to invest a great deal of time in attaining acceptable gifts for Katey.

A primary objective in *Dead Rising 2* is to keep Katey alive by providing her with regular doses of Zombrex (between 7:00 a.m. and 8:00 a.m. every day in the game's fictional time). This suppresses her infection, preventing her from turning into a zombie. Hence, the drug provides a tangible sense of security by offering a legitimate means of prolonging Katey's life. However, the same cannot be said for the gifts needed to obtain the Father of the Month and Father of the Year achievements, which do nothing to sustain Katey's health. In fact, the player's preoccupation with these achievements may even cause Katey to die. By finding gifts for Katey, the player is not actively seeking

Zombrex for her: a task *Dead Rising 2* emphasises. As well as an ever-present counter showing how many doses of Zombrex Chuck possesses at a given time, Chuck is regularly contacted by the supporting character, Stacey, to remind him of Katey's condition. Stacey will call Chuck at 4:00 a.m., 7:00 a.m. and 7:30 a.m. to remind him (and the player) of Katey's medicinal needs. Also, each call is communicated with an increased sense of urgency. Thus, when the player privileges finding gifts for Katey they invoke wasted time. This, in turn produces ludus-based temporal satire targeting their preoccupation with consumer-oriented behaviour. Moreover, this satire serves as another means of deriding the post 9/11 rhetoric of salvation via consumerism discussed in earlier chapters, as no number of toys can save Katey from her infection.

As well as generating ludus-based temporal satire, retail-oriented gameplay objectives can generate paidia-based temporal satire. For example, the fulfilment of *Dead Rising 2*'s Window Shopper achievement requires Chuck to enter every shop in Fortune City. In directing Chuck to do so, the player will inevitably discover many consumer goods throughout *Dead Rising 2*'s traversable areas. Furthermore, the player may become distracted by these goods. Accordingly, Loudermilk's (2003) consumer dementia can be more comprehensively realised by players who forget about both story missions and achievements whilst guiding their avatars through the worlds of *Dead Rising* games – favouring instead the pleasures of retail exploration for its own sake in these worlds. Achievements in *Dead Rising* games can thereby serve as tangential points for players to enter a state of paidia-oriented gameplay. When this occurs, paidia-based temporal satire targeting the player's preoccupation with in-game consumption can be generated.

Paidia-based Temporal Satire

The achievements described above facilitate temporal satire through their encouragement of consumption play that is grounded in realistic consumer activities, such as shopping for clothes and acquiring gifts for a loved one. Adding to this, temporal satire can emerge through the player's sustained effort towards attaining achievements that are concerned with the actualisation of unrealistic consumer desires. Indeed, *Dead Rising* games allow for the actualisation of a specific form of consumer desire that Molesworth and Denegri-Knott (2007) proclaim is especially suited to video games: that of the *fantasy*. This term refers to "speculative ideas that cannot be actualized [in real life], even with unlimited wealth" (Molesworth and Denegri-Knott, 2007: 118). In *Dead Rising* games, players can actualise consumer fantasies that are often alluded to in zombie fictions. Namely, the objectification and subsequent (violent) consumption of the undead. To reiterate, consumption is defined in this book as "using up, destroying, or eating something" (Lehdonvitta et al., 2009: 1062). Thus, zombies are consumed in *Dead Rising* games in the sense that they are destroyed by the player's avatar.

Many achievements in *Dead Rising* games are concerned with killing zombies and crafting weapons. In *Dead Rising 1, 2, 2: Off The Record,* and *3,* respectively, players can gain achievements for killing 53,594 zombies, 72,000 zombies, 100,000 zombies, and 100,004 zombies. Additionally, players can gain achievements for knocking 30 zombies over with a parasol in *Dead Rising 1* and creating combo weapons[4] in *Dead Rising 2, 2: Off The Record,* and *3.* These achievements can pave the way for paidia-based temporal satire as they promote a macabre sense of pleasure that can exist on its own terms, rather than as a by-product of the player fulfilling objectives. Stressing this, Hunt (2015: 116) claims that there is enjoyment to be had in the "excesses and absurdity" of combat in *Dead Rising* games. This is because players can vicariously partake in transgressive behaviours when directing their avatars to attack the undead. Certainly, the destruction of these animated corpses can incite a sadistic sense of enjoyment for players by producing emotionally incongruous experiences for them. Virtual murder – especially that which is spectacular – can be seen as amusing precisely because acts of violence in the real world are generally considered taboo (Bareither, 2017). Indeed, Schott compares the pleasures of playing *Dead Rising 1* with the satisfaction described by *Dawn of the Dead*'s special effects artist, Tom Savini, who described "having so much fun inventing and constructing [the film's various zombie death scenes]" (2011: 147). In *Dead Rising* games, then, visceral consumption play can be gratifying as it is discernibly *splatstick,* meaning that it "presents graphic violence in such an exaggerated way that it becomes a comedic device intentionally played for laughs" (Kroon, 2014: 636).[5]

As addressed in the chapter on spatial satire, an array of consumer items can be used against the undead in *Dead Rising* games. Yet, while these items are generally ineffective against the limitless hordes, they do allow for the destruction of several zombies before they break from overuse. For instance, weapons like chainsaws, spiked bats, and sledge saws (which are made by combining a sledgehammer with cement saw) are more than capable of slaying the undead. Moreover, they allow for the swift killing of zombies in such a way that creates a spectacle by expelling copious amounts of blood from their bodies. Adding to this, certain weapons in *Dead Rising* games can trigger death animations. For example, in *Dead Rising 1, 2, 2: Off The Record* and *3,* shower heads can be lodged into the skulls of zombies. Doing this prompts the creatures to wander around for a few moments as the liquid contents of their bodies spurt from the mechanism in lieu of water. Similarly, buckets filled with drills can be placed onto the heads of zombies like deadly helmets, causing the creatures to be decimated with repeated punctures. As Hunt observes, this method of execution is presented "rather messily" (2015: 117), though it can also be perceived as humorous in its grotesquery. In addition, kill animations can be triggered by players of *Dead Rising 3* after slaughtering several zombies in quick succession (Figure 6.2). When these animations occur, the virtual camera zooms in on the visceral imagery of zombies being torn apart or bludgeoned to death. Crucially,

Figure 6.2 Nick decimates a zombie with a sledge saw in *Dead Rising 3*.

none of these death scenes are required viewing for the player to attain any of the six zombie killing achievements in this game.

Players could slaughter the tens of thousands of zombies required to attain all of the series spanning zombie killing achievements in *Dead Rising* games by simply driving vehicles through crowds of the undead; despite taking up a large portion of each game's fictional time, this would still be the most efficient means of gaining such achievements. Therefore, the spectacular methods of zombie killing included in *Dead Rising* games go beyond story-driven and achievement-driven practicality, establishing tangential opportunities for players to engage in transgressive pleasure through violent gameplay for its own sake. Indeed, the creative ways in which zombies can be destroyed in these games encourages gameplay akin to paidia rather than ludus, as the player is invited to see what they can find to assault the undead and revel in the taboo of causing gratuitous violence. This, of course, uses up valuable fictional time that *Dead Rising* games imply should be dedicated to completing story missions. Therefore, just as ludus-based temporal satire is generated by players participating in consumption play to attain achievements, paidia-based temporal satire is generated by players participating in excessive virtual consumption for their own enjoyment. In both instances, such actions result in a satirisation of the player's temporal investments in simulated consumption when they detract from time-sensitive story missions.

Conclusion

In satirising their players' temporal investments in consumption play, *Dead Rising* games naturalise neoliberal sensibilities. As Bailes remarks, neoliberal subjects are "bombarded from all sides by countless demands from different sources, such as the state, the workplace, our social circles and the media" (2019: 14). Consequently, individuals are expected to excel in all areas of their lives and are deemed personally responsible when they cannot. However, Bailes attests that one would be mistaken in likening the demands of neoliberalism to achieving a "work-life balance," as neoliberal rationalities indicate that no amount of dedication to a single endeavour can ever be enough. Still, in *Dead Rising* games, the idea of balancing these conflicting demands is supported by way of temporal satire.

In *Dead Rising* games, temporal satire only occurs when consumption play eats into fictional time that these games stress should be spent working through story missions, which revolve around their avatar's vocational and parental responsibilities. Thus, it is the player's decision to indulge in *excessive* consumption play is satirised here, not their decision to engage in consumption play (and thereby consumption) in general. In other words, the player's decision to partake in consumption play that disrupts the balance between in-game productivity and consumerist pleasures is satirised. Therefore, *Dead Rising* games legitimise the ideal of a work-life balance by organising designated times for story missions and consumer-oriented activities to take place, while satirising players who "waste" fictional time by having the latter infringe on the former.

To be clear, time wasted engaging in consumption play cannot be attributed to the player's assistance of satirical characters like Luz, Bessie, Rosa, and Erica. Instead, it is time wasted of the player's own volition. This is even the case regarding the player's pursuit of gifts for Chuck's daughter, Katey, who does not ask for these gifts and is unaffected by their presence. Thus, temporal satire in *Dead Rising* games highlights the player's own preoccupation with consumption, not that of in-game agents; it satirises the player's decision to neglect story missions in favour of simulating shopping experiences and, in doing so, encourages self-discipline by means of time management. As a result, *Dead Rising* games legitimise the idea of a sustainable work-life balance besought by neoliberal subjects, even if such a balance is unattainable in the real world "because encoded into the neoliberal ideal of success is a hidden clause that nothing is ever enough" (Bailes, 2019: 14).

While this chapter has focused on the ways in which games construe time as wasteful, and touched briefly on the consequences of wasted time, the next chapter addresses, exclusively and critically, the consequences of the player's gameplay decisions. Certainly, temporal satire can stem from the player's decision to seek out gifts (rather than medicine) for Chuck's infected daughter, but it is consequential satire that arises from the moment of Katey's death should the player let her time run out. To clarify, temporal satire occurs during the moments in which a player is engaged with a video game, alongside the passage of play/fictional time: in the game's *now*, so to speak. Contrastingly, consequential satire occurs when the folly of the player's chosen gameplay style is made clear in the short or long term.[6] So, while temporal satire manifests alongside player actions in *Dead Rising* games, consequential satire stems from the games' reactions to player actions.

Notes

1 For example, in *Animal Crossing: New Horizons* (Nintendo, 2020) an in-game clock parallels real time. Accordingly, the in-game store Nook's Cranny, which is open from 8 a.m. to 10 p.m., is only accessible during this timeslot in real life (providing the player does not alter the time on their Nintendo Switch console).

2 Time progresses much more quickly in *Dead Rising 3*'s "Nightmare Mode." In *Dead Rising 4* there is no in-game timer.

3 Regarding video games, this is an original temporal concept introduced by this research.

4 As their name suggests, combo weapons are created by combining items together.

5 This stresses the necessity of using the concept of *wasted time* in this chapter rather than adopting Juul's *dead time*, as the latter describes gameplay that is boring/uninteresting for the player.

6 This is not to say that temporal satire always anticipates consequential satire, or that consequential satire is necessarily foregrounded by temporal satire.

References

Bailes, J. (2019) *Ideology and the Virtual City: Videogames, Power Fantasies, and Neoliberalism*. Winchester: Zero Books.

Bareither, C. (2017) '"That was so mean :D" – Playful Virtual Violence and the Pleasure of Transgressing Intersecting Emotional Spaces', *Emotion, Space and Society*, 25, pp. 111–18. https://doi.org/10.1016/j.emospa.2016.12.005

Briefel, A. (2011) '"Shop 'Til You Drop!": Consumerism and Horror', in Briefel, A. and Miller, S. J. (eds.) *Horror After 9/11: World of Fear, Cinema of Terror*. Austin: University of Texas Press, pp. 142–62.

Caillois, R. (1961) *Man, Play and* Games. Translated by Meyer Barash. Urbana: University of Illinois Press. Reprinted in 2001.

Consalvo, M. and Dutton, N. (2006) 'Game Analysis: Developing a Methodological Toolkit for the Qualitative Study of Games', *Game Studies*, 6(1). Available at: https://gamestudies.org/0601/articles/consalvo_dutton (Accessed: 15 December 2023).

Frasca, G. (2001) *Videogames of the Oppressed: Videogames as a Means for Critical Thinking and Debate*. Masters degree thesis, Georgia Institute of Technology. Available at: https://ludology.typepad.com/weblog/articles/thesis/ (Accessed: 15 December 2023).

Hunt, N. (2015) 'A Utilitarian Antagonist: The Zombie in Popular Video Games', in Hubner, L., Leaning, M. and Manning, P. (eds.) *The Zombie Renaissance in Popular Culture*. Basingstoke: Palgrave Macmillan, pp. 107–23.

Juul, J. (2004) 'Introduction to Game Time', in Wardrip-Fruin, N. and Harrigan, P. (eds.) *First Person: New Media as Story, Performance, and Game*. Cambridge, MA: MIT Press, pp.131–42.

Juul, J. (2005) *Half-Real: Video Games between Real Rules and Fictional Worlds*. Cambridge, MA: MIT Press.

Kroon, R. W. (2014) *A/V A to Z: An Encyclopedic Dictionary of Media, Entertainment and Other Audiovisual Terms*. Jefferson, NC: McFarland.

Lehdonvitta, V., Wilska, T-A, and Johnson, M. (2009) 'Virtual Consumerism', *Information, Communication & Society*, 12(7), pp. 1059–79. https://doi.org/10.1080/13691180802587813

Loudermilk, A. (2003) 'Eating "Dawn" in the Dark: Zombie Desire and Commodified Identity in George A. Romero's "Dawn of the Dead"', *Journal of Consumer Culture*, 3(1), pp. 83–108. https://doi.org/10.1177/1469540503003001228

Malliet, S. (2007) 'Adapting the Principles of Ludology to the Method of Video Game Content Analysis', *Game Studies*, 7(1). Available at: https://gamestudies.org/0701/articles/malliet (Accessed: 05 December 2023).

Molesworth, M. and Denegri-Knott, J. (2007) 'Digital Play and the Actualization of the Consumer Imagination', *Games and Culture*, 2(2), pp. 114–33. https://doi.org/10.1177/1555412006298209

Newman, J. (2013) *Videogames*. 2nd ed. London: Routledge.

Nitsche, M. (2007) 'Mapping Time in Video Games', in *Proceedings of the 2007 DiGRA International Conference: Situated Play*. Available at: https://www.digra.org/digital-library/publications/mapping-time-in-video-games/ (Accessed: 05 December 2023).

Schott, G. (2011) 'Digital Dead: Translating the Visceral and Satirical Elements of George A. Romero's Dawn of the Dead to Videogames', in Moreman, C. M. and Rushton, C. J. (eds.) *Zombies Are Us: Essays on the Humanity of the Walking Dead*. Jefferson, NC: McFarland, pp. 141–50.

7 Consequential Satire

A significant feature of video games is their ability to provoke decision making among their players. In fact, the primary objective of many game developers is to establish a space where multiple outcomes can arise from the player's input; or, to facilitate *meaningful play* as Salen and Zimmerman (2004) call it. This term describes how meaning "resides in the relationship between action and outcome" (Salen and Zimmerman, 2004: 34). In other words, meaningful play refers to a process wherein a player's in-game actions have noticeable consequences in the form of changes to the game state and the fictional world of a game. The capacity for video games to facilitate such changes often sees them held in opposition to traditional storytelling media – namely, literature and cinema, which typically contain fixed outcomes. By contrast, video games can be categorised by their uncertainty. That is, their potential to convey multiple outcomes that depend, in part or in whole, on the player's actions.

Video games can express satire through the outcomes of players' in-game choices; hence, they can express consequential satire. This form of videoludic satire can manifest in two ways based on whether the satirical outcomes of a player's in-game choices occur immediately or over time. On outcomes to player's in-game choices/actions, Salen and Zimmerman label immediate outcomes *discernible* and outcomes that become apparent over time *integrated.* With the former, a game-system "tells players *what* happened (*I hit the monster*)" whereas with the latter it "lets players know *how* [what happened] will affect the rest of the game (*If I keep on hitting the monster I will kill it. If I kill enough monsters, I'll gain a level.*)" [emphasis in original] (2004: 35). Correspondingly, the term *discernible consequential satire* is used to refer to satirical outcomes that are communicated instantly after the player has made an in-game choice, whereas the term *integrated consequential satire* is used to refer to satirical outcomes that occur sometime after the player has made an in-game choice.

Both forms of consequential satire can be identified using a method of video game analysis called *gameplay logging*, which involves paying close attention to the "emergent aspects of [a] game" (Consalvo and Dutton, 2006: n.p.). For instance, one might seek to document the varying paths a

DOI: 10.4324/9781003467175-8

player can take through game levels and worlds, or perhaps try to push the boundaries of a game by looking for glitches to exploit. In relation to consequential satire, gameplay logging involves documenting the choices that can be made by players during gameplay, as well as their outcomes. Here, gameplay logging focuses on an area of video game analysis that Fernández-Vara calls *choice design* by concentrating on "how the player may be presented with choices and their consequences" (2019: 186). In *Dead Rising* games, the player's choice to partake in "consumption play" (Lehdonvitta et al., 2009: 1061) can be met with satirical outcomes in the form of punishments.

The previous chapter demonstrated how *Dead Rising* games facilitate consumption play while simultaneously centralising story missions concerning their avatars' vocational and parental responsibilities. By doing so, these games present opportunities for players to ignore story missions in favour of pursuing consumption-oriented activities. If the player takes these opportunities, temporal satire becomes apparent due to the contextualisation of consumption play as a waste of time. Following on from this, the current chapter expands on the treatment of consumption play in *Dead Rising* games. This time, with a focus on its outcomes. Accordingly, the first section of this chapter explores decision making in video games to further conceptualise consequential satire. Then, in the second and third sections, discernible consequential satire and integrated consequential satire are exemplified with reference to *Dead Rising* games. In these games, both forms of consequential satire occur when the player's choice to waste time searching for and using up virtual commodities is punished. As shown by way of their analyses, discernible consequential satire and integrated consequential satire legitimises neoliberal ideals in *Dead Rising* games. This is because their associated punishments target acquisitiveness, which, as these games infer, stems from a lack of self-discipline.

Choices and Consequences in Video Games

The importance of player action in video games is addressed by Frasca (2003), who notes the difference between a film about a plane landing and a player controlling a plane in a flight simulation game. The former cannot be manipulated "since film sequences are fixed and unalterable" (Frasca, 2003: 224–5), whereas the latter can. Although, the player's control over aspects of a video game's world, as well as its story-based outcomes, is limited by its design. Hence, the rules of a game, and the developmental routes of its story, are pre-determined by its developers. Yet, the uncertainty regarding how video games can play out provides players with a sense of personal responsibility for what happens in the games that they play. As Isbister asserts, "[a]t the root of the emotional power of games lies the fact that games are comprised of choices with consequences" (2016: 40). This is especially true when players are confronted with, or experience the repercussions of, pivotal moments during gameplay.

It should be noted, however, that explicit consequences stemming from a player's in-game choices are not a prerequisite for the communication of meaning in video games, as is made clear in Telltale's *The Walking Dead* (2012–2019). This video game series originally followed the avatar, Lee Everett, as he struggled to survive in a zombie-infested world. Although, the series eventually centralises Clementine, a young girl who Lee protects in the first game. On a large scale, choices in *The Walking Dead* series are irrelevant, as the world can never be saved from the zombies. Yet, as Stang points out, "the player's choices do influence what kind of person Clementine becomes" (2019: n.p.). Therefore, despite the game's "false choices" (Stang, 2019: n.p.), which carry all players to the same outcome (Lee's death and Clementine's independence), the attitude Clementine adopts can be reflective of the player's morally loaded decisions: who to save, who to abandon, whether to steal supplies from other survivors, for example.

In the second game of Telltale's *The Walking Dead* series, players must decide whether to euthanise a dog after it attacks Clementine. The animal will die either way, but the choice can still be meaningful

> The distinction in Clementine's choice is only relevant to the player's subjective interpretation of the moral character of Clementine. Is she the type of person to prolong a violent dog's suffering? Is it because she is squeamish? Does it come from a place of malice? The player is left to interpret the motive and implications of their choice on their own.
>
> (Nay and Zagal, 2017: n.p.)

Conversely, regarding consequential satire, the player's in-game choices must have explicit outcomes. This is because consequential satire arises from the player's decisions that result in changes to the game state or fictional world of the game being played; it does not arise from the player's implicit and thereby subjective interpretation of the psychology of avatars or agents. In other words, consequential satire is only discernible when the player's choices impact a game in a tangible way. Accordingly, this form of videoludic satire can be read as reflective of the values of game developers, rather than those of game characters. It manifests from the player's decision to pursue actions that game developers anticipate, facilitate, or even invite and deem worthy of punishment and/or ridicule.

Wilcox asserts that video games can satirise their own players by critiquing the choices that these players make during gameplay: a phenomenon he refers to as *ludic satire* (2013). As mentioned in Chapter 1 of this book, Wilcox exemplifies ludic satire by referring to an incident in *Metal Gear Solid 3: Snake Eater*, wherein players can be critiqued for choosing to use lethal rather than non-lethal combat techniques. Yet, as was also mentioned in this chapter, Wilcox's concept has limitations. Notably, it is too restrictive. For Wilcox, ludic satire is only possible in video games that present their players with choices that can lead to positive and negative outcomes. This is debatable, though, as previously argued with reference to Molleindustria's satire on smart phone production, *Phone Story*. Thus, it is important to remember that players do not require in-game choices with strictly positive and negative outcomes to be satirised by game-systems. Moreover, players who are confronted with in-game choices that lead to discernibly satirical outcomes are not always the sole target of a game's satire. Indeed, by means of consequential satire, the *Dead Rising* games satirise the player's choice to prioritise consumption play; but, in doing so, they also satirise excessive consumption more broadly.

Consequential satire stemming from the outcomes of the player's actions demonstrate a clear value judgement on the part of the game-system, whereby players are punished or shamed for choosing to simulate what these systems designate as irresponsible behaviour. Hence, consequential satire becomes apparent when the player's in-game choices are reprimanding by a game-system. There are several ways video games can punish players, all of which may be framed in such a way as to express consequential satire. As detailed in Juul's (2009: 238) taxonomy of video game punishments, video games may utilise the *energy punishment* (by depleting health blocks and bars), the *life punishment* (by taking away an avatar's life, or taking them to a "retry" screen), the *game termination punishment* (by ending the game – this is otherwise known as a "Game Over"), and the *setback punishment* (by forcing the player back to the beginning a level or scenario). Additionally, video games can punish players by subjecting them to the *resource depletion punishment* (when in-game resources are damaged or lost), the *shaming punishment* (when a game-system draws attention to an action that the player has chosen to perform for the purpose of derision), the *unfavourable resolution punishment* (when the resolution of a minor story or quest is negative in some way; this resolution does not end/conclude the game), and the *bad ending punishment* (when the resolution of a game's main story is negative in some way; this resolution ends/concludes the game).[1] Because punishments in video games only occur after players have chosen to make gameplay related choices, they invoke a sense of *complicity* on the part of the player. This term describes how players can feel responsible for the way in-game scenarios unfold (Smethurst and Craps, 2014: 277). Likewise, with regards to the player's in-game choices, Iten *et al.* (2017: 496) state that videogames encourage a sense of responsibility in players, as well as contemplation over which options to pursue. Comparable inferences can be made of consequential satire, which aims to confront players with the stupidity, foolishness, or recklessness of choices they make during gameplay.

In *Dead Rising* games, consequential satire can manifest when players choose to engage in consumption play. As a result, in these games, punishments relating to consumption play evidence a proceduralisation of Romero's satirical film, *Dawn of the Dead*. In Romero's film, Fran and Peter survive due to their shared ability to resist consumer trinkets, unlike Roger and Stephen

(Loudermilk, 2003: 92). Similarly, for players of *Dead Rising* games, the same strength of will must be adopted by players to avoid subjecting their avatars to the same fate as Romero's flawed characters. Furthermore, by targeting the player's choice to partake in consumption play, consequential satire in *Dead Rising* games punishes players for failing to meet the requirements of neoliberal subjectivity. For Baerg, neoliberal subjects must "learn how to make responsible decisions in a context fraught with risk, given the consequences these choices potentially yield" (2012: 157). Moreover, to be a responsible citizen, one must "make choices in keeping with an economically inflected calculative rationality" (Baerg, 2009: 123). This means that choices should be made by closely considering their potential risks/rewards, lest they lead to undesirable/unexpected outcomes. In *Dead Rising* games, choices often concern time and resource management. Hence, the associated punishments of consequential satire in these games stem from the player's inability to utilise their time and resources effectively. Consequential satire therefore not only works to ridicule players for their excessive consumption in *Dead Rising* games, but also to legitimise a neoliberal rationality that views the world through the lens of risk management.

Discernible Consequential Satire

As mentioned in the previous chapter on temporal satire, one way that players of *Dead Rising* games can partake in consumption play is by seeking out and trying on in-game clothing items. These can be found in many shops throughout the Willamette Parkview Mall, Fortune City, Los Perdidos, and Willamette Memorial Megaplex. Contrary to games from *The Legend of Zelda* (Nintendo, 1986 to present) or *World of Warcraft* (Blizzard Entertainment, 2004 to present) series, for example, sampling the various fashions across *Dead Rising* games does nothing to aid in story progression or make gameplay flow more smoothly; clothing items in these games do not increase the avatars' health points, for example. The lack of benefits afforded by clothing items here contributes to an explicit framing of consumption play as a waste of time. Moreover, of significance for this chapter, changing into alternate outfits in *Dead Rising* games can have negative consequences for their avatars, which are made apparent right after these avatars have been commanded to change their clothes.

Changing outfits in *Dead Rising* games puts the avatar in a vulnerable position. This is because, as the avatars alter their attire, their movements can no longer be controlled by players. Instead, an animation sequence takes place wherein Frank, Chuck, and Nick assume temporary autonomy. This animation varies with each game and with the respective clothing items that the avatar is made to change into. For example, in *Dead Rising 1*, Frank will rub his hands together while shuffling his feet when trying on suits, dance provocatively when donning dresses, and jump up and down when changing into childrenswear (Figure 7.1). Crucially, these animation sequences take time. In *Dead Rising 1*, they take between three and ten seconds. In *Dead Rising 2*, *2: Off The Record*, *3*, and *4*, they take around three to six seconds. Although, the latter two games do enable a reduction of these times to approximately two seconds if the player commands their avatars to move as they are shuffling around. However, the couple of seconds it takes to try on new clothes is enough time for zombies to stumble towards the avatar. Therefore, if players do not take the time it takes for their avatars to change clothes into consideration, triggering this action can have disastrous consequences.

In *Dead Rising* games, the avatar's consumption-induced vulnerability can lead to them being assaulted immediately after, or even during, clothing-changing animation sequences.[2] This means that trying on different clothes can lead to an energy punishment in which the avatars' health diminishes as they are attacked by the undead. Moreover, the player's preoccupation with consumption play may lead to a life punishment if avatars are assaulted repeatedly or while they are low on health. In turn, this would trigger the game termination, setback, and resource depletion punishments. This is because avatars in *Dead Rising* games have a single life, with their deaths leading to a Game Over screen. If this occurs, any items the avatar acquired after the player last saved their game is lost. As such, if players of *Dead Rising 1* save their game, explore the mall, have Frank attain weapons and food but then see him killed by zombies, then Frank's collected resources since the player's last save will disappear. Likewise, this pattern of punishments can occur because of the player being distracted by other consumer items. For instance, in *Dead Rising* games, the avatar might be attacked due to the

Figure 7.1 Zombies approach Frank as he changes clothes in *Dead Rising 1*.

player's decision to explore and plunder various stores whilst ignoring the steady progression of the undead towards them.

As with clothing items, the player's (mis)use of certain food items is critiqued by means of discernible consequential satire in *Dead Rising* games. This is communicated when avatars clutch their stomachs in pain or vomit after the player directs them to consume spoiled foods or drink alcohol in excess. As mentioned in Chapter 3 on spatial satire, the capacity of foods and drinks to impede the avatar imbues these objects with affordance-based spatial satire. However, consequential satire is generated by triggering these affordances (purposefully or inadvertently) and suffering the consequences of doing so. Hence, the stomach-clutching and vomiting of avatars convey shaming punishments. This is because these actions visually highlight and satirise the player's choice to make their avatars eat questionable foods or consume more than they need. Likewise, as is the case with many instances of shared satire in *Dead Rising* games, the visualisation of avatar sickness conjures the notions of "ought" and "ought not" referred to by Sherry (1987: 12). Here, a didactic proposition is made whereby the game-system communicates the message that players should not simulate the intake of spoiled food or too much alcohol. Additionally, this constitutes a procedural rhetoric advocating for the player's close consideration of what their avatar eats and drinks.

Punishments for dubious/excessive food intake in *Dead Rising* games are not just communicated via visualisations of avatars in states of illness. In keeping with the consequences of trying on items of clothing, the player's agency is momentarily removed while their avatar doubles over in pain. Moreover, avatars drop any object that they are holding when struck by sickness, thus invoking the resource depletion punishment. Without an object to hold, or the ability for players to control them, avatars are then left open to attack. Truly, it would be particularly detrimental to the avatar's wellbeing if their bout of sickness occurred as the player was leading them through a crowd of zombies. In addition, the act of consuming any food/drink object can prove hazardous in *Dead Rising 1* and *2*. Once the avatar is directed to eat/drink in these games, the selected object will appear in their hands. The avatar will then raise the object to their mouths and bite or gulp it down. Again, the player cannot move their avatar for a couple of seconds while this action occurs, rendering them defenceless and giving ample time for zombies to surround and attack them.

Despite the potential benefits to the avatar's health via eating, stripping the player of agency during food consumption may result in the same pattern of punishments that can be triggered by trying on clothing: these are the energy punishment, life punishment, game termination punishment, and setback punishment. In this way, *Dead Rising* games convey the message that it is unadvisable to eat/drink simply for the sake of eating/drinking by satirising players who command their avatars to do so. To explain further, it is not advisable to consume food/drink for any other reason than to regain the avatar's health in *Dead Rising* games; this, in turn, normalises the notion of living in a perpetual state of risk, while indicating that it is the player's responsibility to manage such risk (by finding safe places for their avatars to eat, not directing them to consume spoiled foods, and moderating their alcohol intake).

Integrated Consequential Satire

Players of *Dead Rising* games can be satirised in the long term for engaging in consumption play. This becomes apparent if they run out of time to complete story missions – if they consistently choose to neglect, or risk not fulfilling, their responsibilities and "waste" time by trying on clothes, exploring shops, and claiming commodities. For example, *Dead Rising 1* and *2* penalise players with unfavourable resolution punishments if they neglect story missions for too long. Unfavourable resolution punishments follow the same pattern in both games. A pop-up notification will label the current and all subsequent story missions "expired," and a caption appears stating that "[t]he truth has vanished into darkness." After this, the player is given the option to load a previous save file, restart the game with their current avatar level intact, or continue playing. The first two options result in game termination, setback, and resource depletion punishments, while the latter inevitably leads to a bad ending punishment. In each game, the bad ending punishment once more emphasises the player's failure to discover the truth behind the zombie outbreak and may even infer the avatar's death. Similarly, if time runs out to complete story missions in *Dead Rising 2: Off The Record* and *3*, bad ending punishments can depict Fortune City and Los Perdidos being bombed before Frank and Nick are able to make their escapes.[3]

Since zombies, although numerous, are not much of an obstacle to gameplay progression in *Dead Rising* games, the possibility of players failing story missions due to assaults from the undead are unlikely. Hence, instances of integrated consequential satire are less liable to be triggered by players losing their battle against the undead than by players who succumb to the detrimental draw of consumption play. This is because a significant portion of gameplay opportunities in these games involve discovering and utilising virtual objects. In fact, the player's decision to waste time engaging in excessive consumption can be explicitly foregrounded in *Dead Rising 2*'s unfavourable resolution punishments. With these punishments, integrated consequential satire stems from the player's decision to dress Chuck in alternate outfits found within Fortune City's many stores. No matter how outlandish these may seem, the clothing items that Chuck is made to wear during gameplay carry over to his depiction in cutscenes. One such example of this can be witnessed in a cutscene that is triggered if the player does not provide Katey with Zombrex, subsequently causing her to turn into a zombie.

Katey's death is presented in two cutscenes. The first occurs when the countdown to deliver Zombrex to her expires and the second occurs if the player returns to Fortune City's emergency shelter after Katey dies. In the first cutscene, the player sees Katey's guardian, Stacey, shift her attention away from a set of computer monitors and towards something that is lurking behind her. Her distraught expression, as well as the gurgling noises heard as she backs away, signify that she is gazing upon an undead Katey. This is confirmed when the statement "KATEY HAS TURNED" appears in bold, red lettering on a black screen. Following this, a visual depiction of all subsequent story missions crossed out with the word "FAILED!" written over them appears onscreen. This does not equate Katey's death with a bad ending punishment, however, as the game session is not terminated once she dies (her death does not result in an immediate "Game Over"). Instead, players can continue to play *Dead Rising 2*, albeit without access to its story missions, until their 72 hours of fictional time expires. Hence, the captions appearing after Katey's death indicate an unfavourable resolution punishment for the player's negligence towards Chuck's daughter.

The first cutscene after Katey's death does not allude to the player's preoccupation with Fortune City fashion, should this preoccupation have been the cause of their failure to protect Chuck's daughter. Though, via its inclusion of the player's avatar, the second cutscene can. In this cutscene, Chuck falls to his knees and punches the ground in frustration upon realising that his daughter is dead. Here, his attire can appear at odds with the gravity of his emotional outburst. As Hunt observes:

> the fact that the player can witness this scene having dressed Chuck in a range of absurd clothing, from women's shoes to a toddler outfit, allows an undermining of the pathos of the scene. Similarly, dressing Chuck in comedic outfits throughout the game does much to undermine the wider sense of threat that we might expect a game associated with horror to contain.
>
> (2015: 118)

While Hunt is correct in pointing out that players can subvert the seriousness of story elements by playing dress up with their avatars in *Dead Rising 2* (and its sequels), he overlooks the satirical potential of enabling the player to change their avatar's clothes. Indeed, the fact that the avatar's alternate attire is made visible while *Dead Rising 2* presents this unfavourable resolution punishment highlights a connection between this attire and the punishment itself. Specifically, it draws attention to the player's choice to neglect Katey in favour of sampling the various fashions that Fortune City has to offer.

Whatever alternate costume Chuck is made to wear serves as a satirical reminder of the player's fixation with excessive consumption: a reminder that is especially significant given the knowledge that the outfits featured in Fortune City are purely cosmetic. As with all *Dead Rising* games, *Dead Rising 2* boasts a variety of clothing items, from tuxedos and hula dresses to cowboy outfits and pyjamas. Accordingly, the player could encounter Katey's death scene in many ways based upon their prior actions in the game. This is demonstrated in Figure 7.2., which shows Chuck (wearing aviator glasses, pink hair, and a plaid suit) moments before finding his daughter dead and consequently suffering a breakdown. Thus, rather than serving strictly to undermine the seriousness of Katey's death, the clothes that the avatar wears conflate Chuck's display of failure and disappointment with the player's choice to indulge in consumption play.

On the player's sense of complicity in video games, Smethurst and Craps explain that "[i]f Mario falls to his death [in *Super Mario Bros.*], it is because of the player's malign intentions or their lack of skill; if he succeeds, it is because the player has navigated him through the game's levels adroitly" (2014: 277). Hence, "when something bad happens to a game character [...] in most cases, it is because of something the player has done or failed to do" (Smethurst and Craps, 2014: 277). To paraphrase Smethurst and Craps, if Katey dies in *Dead Rising 2* it is because of the player's preoccupation with consumption play and their lack of time-management skills. If Katey lives, it is because the player has managed to resist becoming enthralled by the consumer attractions in Fortune City; or, because they have resisted such attractions for just long enough to tend to Katey's needs. Thus, integrated consequential satire in *Dead Rising 2* stresses that consumption play is a choice. Players either strive to obtain Zombrex for Chuck's daughter and manage their time well, or they ignore Chuck's daughter and waste time engaging in consumption play. Accordingly, if something bad happens to Katey, the player only has themselves to blame.

The cutscene in which Chuck breaks down after Katey's death has the potential to satirise the player's trivial gameplay activities, with Chuck's outfit

Figure 7.2 Chuck donning an alternative outfit in *Dead Rising 2*.

functioning as a guilt and regret inducing reminder that the player could have used their time more wisely. Yet, the player can, of course, reload their saved game to a point before Katey dies due to their negligence. As is typical of video games, once the avatar (or in this case, somebody close to them) dies, the player is given the opportunity to reload a previous save file. Indeed, writing on how video games bestow players with the power of temporal control by enabling them to pause and save their progress, Hanson states that game mechanics give players "the ability to revisit the same challenges repeatedly and without consequence" (2018: 198). However, saving in *Dead Rising 2* (and other games in the *Dead Rising* series) does have consequences, particularly if the player has privileged consumption play over the completion of story missions.[4]

Saving after engaging in consumption play in *Dead Rising 2* may lead to the unavoidability of Katey's death. This, of course, would be satirical due to the knowledge that such a scenario could have been avoided if the player had resisted the temptations of Fortune City's consumption-based environments and managed their time more efficiently. Thus, in addition to having the potential to satirise the player's consumption-oriented gameplay, the unfavourable resolution punishment of Katey's death perpetuates a notion that Baerg states can be found among video games more broadly in that it "naturalizes a risk-management approach to the contemporary situation" (2009: 123). According to Baerg, video games legitimise neoliberal rationalities that are grounded in risk management by "invoking the instrumentality of numbers in their various guises" (2009: 123). In *Dead Rising 2*, with regards to the delivery of Katey's Zombrex and other key objectives, quantitative information in the form of *time* is used to indicate risks to the safety of in-game characters, as well as how sufficiently the player is coping with such risks (do they have enough time to complete certain tasks, for example).

As mentioned earlier, if Katey dies in *Dead Rising 2* all subsequent story missions in the game become unavailable. Therefore, in satirising the player's decision to risk Katey's life by participating in consumption play, *Dead Rising 2* uses the quantifiable variable of time to promote a neoliberal subjectivity grounded in risk management. As Baerg argues of other video games revolving around quantifiable variables – such as *Killzone 2* (Sony Computer Entertainment, 2009) which uses "numerical data to discern a given weapon's efficiency" (2009: 124) – players are not forced to make prudent decisions in *Dead Rising 2*. However, "failing to act responsibly inevitably leads to a failure to win or potentially a failure to enjoy the digital game experience and accrue the benefits that derive from victory and/or participation" (Baerg, 2009: 124). Concerning *Dead Rising 2*, failing to meet the requirements of story missions like keeping Katey alive leads to a failure to experience the full scope of the game's story. This means that, in satirising the player's inability to manage their time properly, *Dead Rising 2* encourages a calculative rationality based on the time-based management of its gameplay activities.

Conclusion

Dead Rising games evidence consequential satire by presenting players with choices: should they prioritise story missions or should they engage in consumption play at the expense of these missions? If players select the latter option, they are punished by the game-systems. Punishments can occur immediately after the player chooses to engage in consumption play via their avatar's loss of health, their loss of life, or their loss of resources. Alternatively, punishments can occur sometime after the player chooses to engage in consumption play via the unfolding of story-related scenarios that are undesirable. As punishments are tied to the player's choice to engage in consumption play, they reveal the value systems inherent in *Dead Rising* games. Specifically, they reveal that these games portray unchecked consumption as worthy of chastisement and ridicule by way of consequential satire. Satirical punishments in *Dead Rising* games thereby proceduralise the logic inherent in Romero's *Dawn of the Dead*. That is, they cynically conclude the consumption-oriented pleasures of these games, which are akin to what Loudermilk (2003) calls Mall Fantasia, by revealing excessive consumption to be harmful to both their avatars and those around them.

Consequential satire consolidates several neoliberal values that have been expressed through other modes of videoludic satire in *Dead Rising* games. By satirising excessive consumption, the neoliberal values legitimised in *Dead Rising* games include self-discipline and resource management. Both values convey the idea that players are *responsible* for their situations, no matter how outlandish these situations may be. This sense of responsibility is emphasised by consequential satire, especially when this mode of videoludic satire manifests via punishments to consumption play that detracts from the avatar's responsibilities. For example, shared satire might infer that the player should not endanger themselves or waste time being preoccupied with material goods through the actions of Luz, Bessie, Rosa, and Erica. Yet, it is consequential satire that makes this more explicit and personal by satirising the actions of the player directly.

Consequential satire in *Dead Rising* games asserts that the player should control their consumer impulses and managed their time/resources efficiently. Although, this is not to say that players of *Dead Rising* games are discouraged from enjoying in-game consumption altogether. *Dead Rising* games legitimise the key demand of neoliberalism to "enjoy responsibly" (Bailes, 2019: 20). This demand was outlined in the previous chapter on temporal satire, where it was evidenced in *Dead Rising* games via their inclusion of interim periods between story missions: time in which players can engage in consumption play that does not have narrative repercussions in the sense that missions cannot be failed as none are active.[5] Consequential satire thereby rationalises the neoliberal demand to enjoy responsibly because its associated punishments arise from consumption play that is either irresponsible or occurs during times where story missions are active. In this way, *Dead Rising* games do not oppose consumption. Instead, they problematises excessive consumption: that which detracts from their avatar's responsibilities.

Notes

1 The latter four punishments are original concepts in this research that have been added to Juul's list, which does not encompass the full range of punishments utilised in video games. Taken together, the punishments outlined here cover the breadth of ways that consequential satire can manifest as outcomes to in-game choices made by video game players.

2 In *Dead Rising 1*, zombies cannot attack the avatar while he changes clothes. Instead, they attack immediately after the animation sequence has finished. In latter games, zombies can assault the avatar while they are changing clothes.

3 As *Dead Rising 4* has no timer system, there are no bad ending punishments related to the player's failure to manage their time efficiently in this game.

4 *Dead Rising 2* and *2: Off The Record* have a limited number of save slots (three to be exact), meaning that players must be careful when deciding whether to save their game. Equally, players of *Dead Rising 1* must be more wary of saving, as the original Xbox 360 version of the game has only one save slot. As such, while "[t]here are a lot of places to explore and a lot of things to try in the game [...] the save structure makes experimentation very costly" (Herold, 2006: n.p.). Consequently, if players save their games with little time to complete story objectives, they risk having to start their games over to fully experience their stories. On the contrary, *Dead Rising 3* has a chapter select option, so players are not forced to restart their entire game if they do not manage their time well. Likewise, *Dead Rising 4* has a chapter selection option too, but the player would not need to use this for any reason relating to time management as there is no timer in this game.

5 The player can, of course, still be killed during these interim periods if they are not careful.

References

Baerg, A. (2009) 'Governmentality, Neoliberalism, and the Digital Game', *Symplokē*, 17(1–2), pp. 115–27. Available at: https://www.jstor.org/stable/10.5250/symploke.17.1-2.0115 (Accessed: 01 December 2023).

Baerg, A. (2012) 'Risky Business: Neo-liberal Rationality and the Computer RPG', in Voorhees, G. A., Call, J. and Whitlock, K. (eds.) *Dungeons, Dragons, and Digital Denizens: The Digital Role-Playing Game*. New York: Bloomsbury, pp. 152–73.

Bailes, J. (2019) *Ideology and the Virtual City: Videogames, Power Fantasies, and Neoliberalism*. Winchester: Zero Books.

Consalvo, M. and Dutton, N. (2006) 'Game Analysis: Developing a Methodological Toolkit for the Qualitative Study of Games', *Game Studies*, 6(1). Available at: https://gamestudies.org/0601/articles/consalvo_dutton (Accessed: 15 December 2023).

Fernández-Vara, C. (2019) *Introduction to Game Analysis*. 2nd edn. New York: Routledge.

Frasca, G. (2003) 'Simulation versus Narrative: Introduction to Ludology', in Wolf, M. J. P. and Perron, B. (eds.) *The Video Game Theory Reader*. London: Routledge, pp. 221–35.

Hanson, C. (2018) *Game Time: Understanding Temporality in Video Games*. Bloomington: Indiana University Press.

Herold, C. (2006) 'The Mall Is an Armory Where Zombies Roam', *The New York Times*, August 24. Available at: https://www.nytimes.com/2006/08/24/technology/24game.html (Accessed: 1 December 2023).

Hunt, N. (2015) 'A Utilitarian Antagonist: The Zombie in Popular Video Games', in Hubner, L., Leaning, M. and Manning, P. (eds.) *The* Zombie *Renaissance in Popular Culture*. Basingstoke: Palgrave Macmillan, pp. 107–23.

Isbister, K. (2016) *How Games Move Us: Emotion by Design*. Cambridge, MA: MIT Press.

Iten, G. H., Steinemann, S. T. and Opwis, K. (2017) 'To Save or To Sacrifice? – Understanding Meaningful Choices in Games', in *Extended Abstracts Publication of the Annual Symposium on Computer-Human Interaction* in Play, pp. 495–502. https://doi.org/10.1145/3130859.3131309

Juul, J. (2009) 'Fear of Failing? The Many Meanings of Difficulty in Video Games', in Perron, B. and Wolf, M. J. P. (eds.) *The Video Game Theory Reader 2*. London: Routledge, pp. 237–52.

Lehdonvitta, V., Wilska, T.-A. and Johnson, M. (2009) 'Virtual Consumerism', *Information, Communication & Society*, 12(7), pp. 1059–79. https://doi.org/10.1080/13691180802587813

Loudermilk, A. (2003) 'Eating "Dawn" in the Dark: Zombie Desire and Commodified Identity in George A. Romero's "Dawn of the Dead"', Journal *of Consumer Culture*, 3(1), pp. 83–108. https://doi.org/10.1177/1469540503003001228

Nay, J. L. and Zagal, J. P. (2017) 'Meaning without Consequence: Virtue Ethics and Inconsequential Choices in Games', in *Proceedings of the 12th International Conference on the Foundations of Digital Games*, pp. 1–8. https://doi.org/10.1145/3102071.3102073

Salen, K. and Zimmerman, E. (2004) *Rules of Play: Game Design Fundamentals*. Cambridge, MA: MIT Press.

Sherry, J. (1987) 'Four Modes of Caricature: Reflections upon a Genre', *Bulletin of Research in the Humanities*, pp. 1–42. Available at: https://jim-sherry.com/caricature.pdf (Accessed: 11 December 2023).

Smethurst, T. and Craps, S. (2014) 'Playing with Trauma: Interreactivity, Empathy, and Complicity in *The Walking Dead* Video Game', *Games* and *Culture*, 10(3), pp. 269–90. https://doi.org/10.1177/1555412014559306

Stang, S. (2019) '"This Action Will Have Consequences": Interactivity and Player Agency', *Game Studies*, 19(1). Available at: https://gamestudies.org/1901/articles/stang (Accessed: 18 December 2023).

Wilcox, S. (2013) 'From Monopoly to Metal Gear: A Survey of Ludic Satire', *First Person Scholar*, 25 September. Available at: https://www.firstpersonscholar.com/from-monopoly-to-metal-gear/ (Accessed: 01 December 2023).

Conclusion

In Loudermilk's appraisal of George A. Romero's *Dawn of the Dead*, he argues that the film's satirical analogy between zombies and consumers has "become 'unmoored' from its original context and appropriated by the very consumer/capitalist society it sought to subvert" (2003: 95). Hence, Loudermilk argues that popular cultural allusions to Romero's film are typically devoid of countercultural implications; instead of furthering the film's criticality of consumer culture, these imitations merely seek to capitalise on the satire of *Dawn of the Dead*. Evidencing this, Loudermilk cites "rip-offs" of Romero's film as well as popular cultural references to it, like *City of the Walking Dead* (Lenzi, 1980) and the "Treehouse of Horror III" episode of *The Simpsons* (Fox, 1989 to present). Crucially, neither of these texts transcends simply reiterating the crux of Romero's film: that capitalism instils within people a zombie-like desire to consume. Accordingly, for Loudermilk, *Dawn of the Dead* has come to embody "an anti-commodity serially re-commodified into an ideological trend" (2003: 98). Certainly, *Dead Rising* games can be situated among the numerous texts capitalising on the success of Romero's film. Yet, these games are also distinguishable from other imitations of Romero's work because – rather than simply re-addressing, and thereby diluting, the satire on consumerism featured in *Dawn of the Dead* – they seize the countercultural essence of Romero's satire and repurpose it to solidify hegemonic ideals.

Applying this book's taxonomy of videoludic satire to *Dead Rising* games has allowed for misconceptions relating to these games to be challenged. Perhaps the most obvious misconception is that "the point of playing the games is to shoot zombies, not understand a character's persona" (Wetmore, Jr., 2011: 101). This is, of course, untrue. In fact, in *Dead Rising* games guns are relatively sparse compared to other objects, like household decorations and toys. Moreover, understanding the mindsets of characters in *Dead Rising* games is crucial in comprehending their narratives, as well as their satirisations of excessive consumption. More significantly, though, the analyses presented in this book call into question readings of the first *Dead Rising game* by Schott (2011) and Weise (2009; 2011). For Schott, the multitude of easily accessible commodities throughout *Dead Rising 1* ensures that this

DOI: 10.4324/9781003467175-9

game simulates consumerism in an idealised manner, wherein players can fulfil their consumer desires unproblematically. Hence, Schott views *Dead Rising 1* in opposition to *Dawn of the Dead*, claiming that "while the notion of mall-as-utopia is a flawed one for the characters in [Romero's film], it works effectively for the player of [Capcom's game] engaging in consumption as play" (2011: 147). On the contrary, Weise (2009; 2011) posits that *Dead Rising 1* problematises consumerism and, by extension, Western capitalist principles by devaluing luxury goods. Indeed, in this game and its sequels, items that symbolise wealth (like jewellery and ornaments) become less valuable than those with a practical use against in-game enemies (like chainsaws and swords). Crucially, as this book has demonstrated, the points made by Schott and Weise can be synthesised by examining *Dead Rising* games through analytical lenses that centralise each form of videoludic satire.

By paying close attention to the videoludic satire expressed in *Dead Rising* games, it is made clear that *Dead Rising 1* and its sequels enable, and even encourage, players to indulge in consumer pleasure, while ensuring that such indulgences are *not* experienced unconditionally and without consequences. Examinations of videoludic satire in these games prove that, from an ideological standpoint, their satirisations of excessive consumption are dissimilar to Romero's satirisation of American consumer culture in *Dawn of the Dead*. Therefore, *Dead Rising 1* does not fully "embrace counter-cultural thinking" (Weise, 2011: 166), and neither do its sequels. Rather, *Dead Rising* games are ideologically conservative in their legitimisation of hegemonic ideals, which can best be described as neoliberal. In short, while *Dawn of the Dead* can be considered subversive due to its satire on consumer culture, the satire of *Dead Rising* games is discernibly conservative in its appropriation of Romero's filmic satire to advocate neoliberal ideals: such as individualism, self-discipline, the ability to manage resources and risk, and a work-life-balance that allows for the maximisation of both leisure activities and vocational (or other) responsibilities.

Beyond *Dead Rising*: Wider Applications for the Taxonomy of Videoludic Satire

This book's taxonomy of videoludic satire affords a necessary flexibility in approaching satire in video games. Not all its forms need to be present, or present to the same degree, in a video game for that game to be read as satirical. This has been illustrated with regards to *Dead Rising* games, as temporal satire is present in *Dead Rising 1*, *2*, *2: Off The Record*, and *3*, but is absent from *Dead Rising 4*. This does not mean that *Dead Rising 4* is lacking in satiric potential, though, as the use of spatial satire and auditory satire are especially prominent in this game. Likewise, temporal satire and consequential satire are missing from Molleindustria's *Phone Story*, which was addressed in Chapter 1 of this book. Yet, this does not mean that *Phone Story* fails to satirise both the unethical processes involved in smart phone production and the player's inferred complicity with these processes. On the contrary, the game communicates its satire through parodic allusions to Apple products, in-game characters, and voice-over narration that encourages its players to consider the ethics of their gaming platform. In other words, it conveys its satire in the form of spatial satire, shared satire, and auditory satire.

The taxonomy of videoludic satire can be used to illuminate scholarly understandings of satirical video games. For example, Wilcox states that the *Farmville* (Zynga, 2009) inspired Facebook game *Cow Clicker* (Bogost, 2010) "is not so much a commentary on Zynga games as it is a critique of an individual who has the time, resources, and desire to perform a simple, repetitive task for arbitrary rewards" (2013). Certainly, as the game merely consists of clicking a virtual cow once every six hours in real-time to gain points, an obvious form of videoludic satire expressed in *Cow Clicker* is temporal satire. Specifically, ludus-based temporal satire, as the player's time is arguably wasted in pursuit of the singular goal of clicking cows (there is nothing else to do in this game other than accumulate points when an ever-present timer diminishes, allowing a cow to be clicked). So, most of the time the player spends within the game is fruitless – it is *destroyed time*, as Bogost (2010) would call it. Yet, *Cow Clicker*'s satirisation of Zynga-style games should not so easily be side-lined, especially as Bogost states that his game is "a Facebook game about Facebook games" (2023: n.p.).

By applying the taxonomy of videoludic satire to *Cow Clicker* the extent to which the game satirises Zynga-style games becomes clear. In fact, observations made about *Cow Clicker* by Tyler (2015) can be expanded upon using the taxonomy of videoludic satire. Specifically, Tyler argues that *Cow Clicker*'s minimalistic, if not crude, visual style distils the essence of games like *Farmville* to highlight the "soulless inanity of our experience when playing them" (2015: 204). For instance, the plain, two-toned "pastures" on which the cows appear (an example of spatial satire) and the player's limited interaction with the game's animals (an example of shared satire) constitute a satiric *reductio as absurdum* of Facebook games (Tyler, 2015: 204). Furthermore, Tyler observes that *Cow Clicker*'s multitude of visually distinct cows, which players can unlock, are "functionally identical [to the game's standard cows]" (Tyler, 2015: 204). Hence, he associates the satire of these unlockable animals to their inability to alter gameplay in any way. Here, Tyler's observations constitute an examination of *Cow Clicker*'s unlockable animals as *game pieces*, as they focus on how the player can interact with these animals. However, by drawing on notions of shared satire, more can be said of these creatures as *fictional beings*: as representational objects with satiric implications.

Players of *Cow Clicker* begin their game with a Plain Cow: a crudely drawn cow that is white in colour. Additional cows can be bought with the game's virtual currency, which is aptly named "Mooney." These animals are available in different colours (like Yellow Cows and Purple Cows) and breeds (like Red Poll

Cows and Highland Cows). Other cows allude to popular commodities, like the bejewelled Rhinestone Cow and the Hello Cow, which parodies Sanrio's Hello Kitty character. In addition, *Cow Clicker* boasts a golden-coloured Bling Cow, which has a nose ring and eyes that appear to be made of diamonds. The selling price for the Bling Cow is 10,000 Mooney: approximately 80 dollars given that 2,500 Mooney equated to around 20 dollars (Alexander, 2011). Notably, the appearances of the Rhinestone Cow, Hello Cow, and Bling Cow allude to valued and valuable commodities. Thus, a disconnect is created between their inferred, culturally situated worth and their gameplay functionality – which is indistinguishable from that of the standard Plain Cow.

The disconnect between the inferred worth and non-distinct functionality of purchasable cows in *Cow Clicker* enhances what the game suggests is the superficiality of Facebook games. Despite their varied looks, they are essentially the same. All are "mere objects of your clicks" (Tyler, 2015: 204). Awareness of the game's cows as fictional beings therefore enhances, and even contextualises, their satire as game pieces. Moreover, the pricing of these cows, which spans between 200 Mooney and 100,000 Mooney, arguably constitutes criticism of a gaming culture now saturated by microtransactions (in-game purchases). As such, *Cow Clicker* does not just satirise the dedication of its players to completing monotonous tasks (Wilcox, 2013) and the minimalism of gameplay in Zynga games (Tyler, 2015). The game also satirises the willingness of players to part with real money for immaterial goods. By facilitating monetary exchanges, then, *Cow Clicker* allows for consequential satire. Specifically, consequential satire characterised by the resource depletion punishment. Only this time, it is not just in-game resources that are depleted, such as the loss of virtual currency in *Dead Rising* games. Instead, it is the player's *real* money that is depleted. Thus, applying the taxonomy of videoludic satire to *Cow Clicker* reveals an expansion of its targets of satire from those highlighted by Wilcox and Tyler.

The Future of Videoludic Satire

In anticipation of future research on satire in games, it is worth mentioning a brief instance where satire can be seen to stem from the player's physical actions in *Dead Rising 3*. During the battle between the avatar and this game's primary representation of gluttony, Darlene Fleischermacher, the player can taunt Darlene by utilising the Xbox's Kinect. Released in 2010, the Kinect is a motion-sensing device that recognises voice commands. In *Dead Rising 3*, each psychopath has a trigger phrase that the player can shout. When these are recognised by the Kinect, psychopaths become flustered and, consequently, vulnerable to the avatar's attacks. Darlene's trigger phrase is "I'm hungry!" – a statement she exclaims with zest in her introductory cutscene. Therefore, in an instance of *kinetic gestural interaction*, wherein "the *player* [...] bodily participates with the sound on screen" [emphasis in original] (Collins, 2008: 127), players of *Dead Rising 3* can vocally mock Darlene's unchecked appetite to throw her off guard.

As well as benefitting the player from a gameplay perspective, verbally taunting Darlene results in the player partaking in the satirical technique of superiority. As outlined by Feinberg (1967: 206), this technique is apparent when an audience is invited to look down on a target of satire. In the case of *Dead Rising 3*, the player is invited to look down on Darlene by mocking her gluttonous behaviour. However, in mocking Darlene, the player also imitates her. As such, *Dead Rising 3* could also be seen to satirise the player by having them loudly exclaim that they are hungry in a manner that is reminiscent of Darlene's aggressive shouting. Here, the player can unwittingly become an object of derision by figuratively adopting Darlene's negative traits and appearing like a glutton themselves. This could be considered another manifestation of shared satire (in its competitive form alongside the other ways the player can combat Darlene), or even a broadening of auditory satire (by considering sounds made *outside* of games). Alternatively, it may indicate an additional form of videoludic satire: perhaps *kinaesthetic satire*. This speculative mode of videoludic satire could be modelled after Calleja's concept of kinaesthetic involvement, which "relates to all modes of avatar or game piece control in virtual environments, ranging from learning controls to the fluency of internalized movement" (2011: 43). Like kinesthetic involvement, then, additional forms of videoludic satire could be attentive to the ways in which player's assert control in video games: by button pushing, swinging remotes, moving their bodies, and voicing commands. Indeed, while arguing that *Grand Theft Auto V* satirises the American Dream,[1] Wills hints at a tactile form of video game satire wherein "sensations from the controller [...] playfully [mimic] drug used, reckless driving and fist fighting" (2021: 3).

As with the Kinect, the development of new gaming technologies may also bring with them new avenues through which videoludic satire can be communicated. For instance, Samurai Punk's *The American Dream* (2018) shows that VR gaming can be adopted for the purpose of satire with its sardonic glorification of firearm ownership. Also, in communicating its satire, the game provides another potential example of kinesthetic satire. Using the Oculus Touch (2016) and Sony's PlayStation Move (2010) motion controllers to simulate the act of shooting, *The American Dream* necessitates the use of virtual guns in its simulations of domestic chores, recreational activities, and work. Although the game's commitment to motion controls could be viewed from a purely practical perspective: the incorporation of the player's bodily movements (beyond moving joysticks and pushing buttons) may serve more as an intriguing novelty for gameplay, rather than a thorough attempt at emphasising its satire on the normalisation of gun proprietorship in the United States. Nonetheless, alongside the development of new gaming technologies comes the *potential* for new forms of videoludic satire to be communicated.

Furthermore, with industry members anticipating an increasing conflation between the real and the virtual in the coming decade (Shea, 2020), the possibilities for videoludic satire could be limitless.

By conceptualising spatial satire, shared satire, auditory satire, temporal satire, and consequential satire, this book has presented a range of research methods to better understand and examine videoludic satire. Moreover, in applying these research methods to Capcom's *Dead Rising* games among others, it has shown the value of its taxonomy of videoludic satire in determining what video games satirise and how they communicate their satire. Likewise, by establishing and exemplifying its classifications of videoludic satire, this book has shown how analyses of videoludic satire can lead to ideologically grounded, interpretative analyses of video game texts. As such, the taxonomy of videoludic satire detailed in these pages provides researchers with a means of deciphering the rhetorics at play within satirical video games, thereby opening the door for future research on videoludic satire.

Note

1 The American Dream refers to the "ideal that the United States is a land of opportunity that allows the possibility of upward mobility, freedom, and equality for people of all classes who work hard and have the will to succeed" (Murtoff, 2023).

References

Alexander, L. (2011) 'The Life-Changing $20 Rightward-Facing Cow', *Kotaku*, 3 October. Available at: https://kotaku.com/the-life-changing-20-rightward-facing-cow-5846080 (Accessed: 20 December 2023).

Bogost, I. (2010) 'Cow Clicker: The Making of Obsession', *Ian Bogost*, 21 July. Available at: https://bogost.com/blog/cow_clicker_1/ (Accessed: 20 December 2023).

Bogost, I. (2023) 'Cow Clicker: A Facebook Game about Facebook Games', *Ian Bogost*. Available at: https://bogost.com/games/cow_clicker/ (Accessed: 20 December 2023).

Calleja, G. (2011) *In-Game: From Immersion to Incorporation*. Cambridge, MA: MIT Press.

Collins, K. (2008) *Game Sound: An Introduction to the History, Theory, and Practice of Video Game Music and Sound Design*. Cambridge, MA: MIT Press.

Feinberg, L. (1967) *Introduction to Satire*. Reprint 2008. Santa Fe, New Mexico: Pilgrims Process, Inc.

Loudermilk, A. (2003) 'Eating "Dawn" in the Dark: Zombie desire and commodified identity in George A. Romero's "Dawn of the Dead"', *Journal of Consumer Culture*, 3(1), pp. 83–108. https://doi.org/10.1177/1469540503003001228

Murtoff, J. (2023) 'American Dream', *Encyclopedia Britannica*, 16 November. Available at: https://www.britannica.com/topic/American-Dream (Accessed: 20 December 2023).

Schott, G. (2011) 'Digital Dead: Translating the Visceral and Satirical Elements of George A. Romero's Dawn of the Dead to Videogames', in Moreman, C. M. and

Rushton, C. J. (eds.) *Zombies Are Us: Essays on the Humanity of the Walking Dead.* Jefferson, NC: McFarland, pp. 141–50.

Shea, C. (2020) 'The Games Industry on What Gaming Might Be Like in 2030', *IGN*, 24 June. Available at: https://www.ign.com/articles/the-games-industry-on-what-gaming-might-be-like-in-2030 (Accessed: 20 December 2023).

Tyler, T. (2015) 'Cows, Clicks, Ciphers, and Satire', *NECSUS: European Journal of Media Studies*, 4(1), pp. 199–208. https://doi.org/10.25969/mediarep/15180

Weise, M. (2009) 'The Rules of Horror: Procedural Adaptation in Clock Tower, Resident Evil, and Dead Rising', in Perron, B. (ed.) *Horror Video Games: Essays on the Fusion of Fear and Play*. Jefferson, NC: McFarland, pp. 238–66.

Weise, M. J. (2011) 'How the Zombie Changed Videogames', in Moreman, C. M. and Rushton, C. J. (eds.) *Zombies Are Us: Essays on the Humanity of the Walking Dead.* Jefferson, NC: McFarland, pp. 151–68.

Wetmore, Jr. K. J. (2011) Back from the Dead: Remakes of the Romero Zombie Films as Markers of Their Times. Jefferson, NC: McFarland.

Wilcox, S. (2013) 'From Monopoly to Metal Gear: A Survey of Ludic Satire', *First Person Scholar*, 25 September. Available at: https://www.firstpersonscholar.com/from-monopoly-to-metal-gear/ (Accessed: 01 December 2023).

Wills, J. (2021) '"Ain't the American Dream Grand": Satirical Play in Rockstar's Grand Theft Auto V', *European Journal of American Studies*, 16(3), pp. 1–16. https://doi.org/10.4000/ejas.17274

Index

For Product Safety Concerns and Information please contact our EU representative GPSR@taylorandfrancis.com
Taylor & Francis Verlag GmbH, Kaufingerstraße 24, 80331 München, Germany

www.ingramcontent.com/pod-product-compliance
Lightning Source LLC
LaVergne TN
LVHW010931110826
845149LV00013B/2546

* 9 7 8 1 0 3 2 7 4 0 0 3 4 *